Fun & Easy

American History
☆ Crafts and Games ☆

by Rhonda Lucas Donald

SCHOLASTIC
PROFESSIONAL BOOKS

New York ◆ Toronto ◆ London ◆ Auckland ◆ Sydney ◆ Mexico City ◆ New Delhi ◆ Hong Kong ◆ Buenos Aires

Dedication

To my sister, Kimberly—
thanks for all your help.

Cover design by Norma Ortiz

Interior design by Ellen Matlach Hassell
for Boultinghouse & Boultinghouse, Inc.

Interior illustrations by Manuel Rivera

ISBN 0-439-17032-X

Contents

Introduction

How to Use This Book

This book is divided into six sections that range from pre-Colonial America to World War II. In each section you'll find a time line of important dates and events, a brief overview of the period covered, and several crafts and activities designed to help your students experience what life might have been like for the people living in each period. Among the crafts are things that people would have made as necessities of everyday life or that would have been typical for the time. These may have been items that people needed but couldn't always buy. You'll also find activities that can help students better understand some aspect of each period. For example, learning about mapmaking will help students appreciate the importance of cartographic skills when people were first exploring the vastly uncharted West. Toys and games are also included to give students an idea of leisure-time activities. Finally, you'll find a recipe from each period. Making and sharing these foods will give your students a real "taste" of history.

Craft Materials to Suit Your Classroom

Note that the crafts are not made with authentic period materials. Instead they feature materials that are easily obtainable and made from recycled objects whenever possible. What you don't already have on hand can, in many cases, be brought from home or purchased inexpensively from a craft store.

Don't Stop Your Studies!

Just because this book stops with World War II doesn't mean your exploration of history has to. Build upon the ideas in this book to extend your studies from the 1950s into the present. Create your own time line of dates and events. And come up with craft and activity ideas to fit the times. Older relatives make great resources for studying this time period. You can have students interview them or invite seniors to visit your class and share their experiences and answer students' questions. Think about the history you and your students are making today. Consider putting together a time capsule and set a date to open it and explore what it reveals about the time it was created.

Early America: Land of Native Peoples

Although the Pleistocene Ice Age ended some 10,000 to 40,000 years ago, the cold climate cooperated long enough to allow groups of Asian people from Siberia to cross what is now the Bering Strait and enter North America. At that time, scientists believe animals and people could have crossed on dry land or perhaps over solid ice. Later with warmer temperatures and higher water levels, the existing land bridge was flooded over by the rising ocean. Today the Bering Strait separates Siberia from Alaska.

Following mammoth and bison herds, the people eventually spread across all of North, Central, and South America. By the time European explorers arrived in the late fifteenth and early sixteenth centuries, there were 10 million people making up hundreds of Indian groups throughout all of North America.

Native Americans enjoyed diverse cultures. Some were farmers who lived in villages, others were nomadic hunters who moved with the animals they preyed upon. All Native Americans were spiritual people who revered nature. They did not have a written language, but they passed down their beliefs and history from generation to generation by telling stories. Early North American cultures were divided into groups based on the region of the country in which they lived and their particular lifestyles. Examples of North and Northeastern groups are the Algonquian, Delaware, Chippewa, Illinois, and Ojibway. Southeastern groups include the Cherokee, Choctaw, Natchez, and Seminole. Plains Indians include the Blackfoot, Cheyenne, Crow, Nez Percé, and Sioux. Indians of the Southwest include the Apache, Navajo, Pueblo, and Yuma.

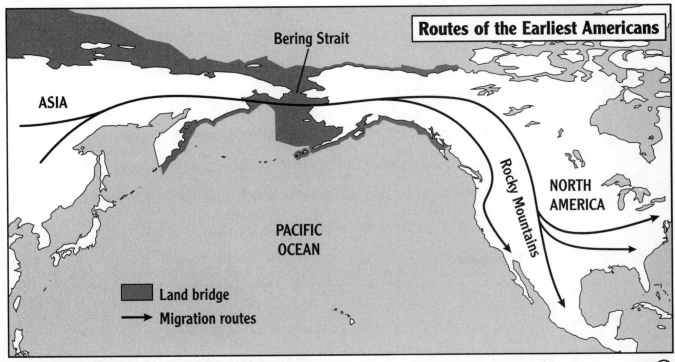

Routes of the Earliest Americans

Bering Strait

ASIA

Rocky Mountains

NORTH AMERICA

PACIFIC OCEAN

Land bridge
Migration routes

The Chinook, Duwamish, Tlingit, and Yakima are examples of Northwest groups.

The arrival of European explorers such as Christopher Columbus and Hernándo Cortés drastically changed the lives of American Indians. When Europeans arrived, the Indians at first welcomed them and even helped them survive. Squanto, for example, taught Pilgrims in Plymouth how to hunt, fish, and grow corn. But explorers and colonists believed they had the right to take whatever they wanted in the "New World," and they began claiming more and more land, thus encroaching on the native people. In 1754, many Indian groups joined with the French in a war against British soldiers and American colonists. Britain and France were already fighting in Europe, so the war in North America was an extension of this conflict. Additionally, Americans wanted to settle on French lands and take advantage of the rich natural resources there. When Britain won the war in 1763, it gained Canada and all land east of the Mississippi River. Several years later, colonists began pushing Native Americans even farther west. By 1853, the U.S. government had taken all of what is now the lower 48 states from its original inhabitants. Today most of the 2 million American Indians live on reservations established by the federal government.

Time Line

30,000 to 10,000 years ago Asian people from Siberia cross a land bridge in what is now the Bering Strait into North America

4000 years ago People in the Americas begin to domesticate and grow corn

A.D. 900 Anasazi build elaborate cliff dwellings in the Southwest

1492 Christopher Columbus arrives in North America

1565 Spanish city of St. Augustine, Florida, founded

1587 English colony on Roanoke Island in Virginia founded

1607 First permanent English colony founded at Jamestown, Virginia

1619 First Africans brought to America as slaves

1620 Pilgrims land in Cape Cod Bay and name the site Plymouth

1732 The thirteenth British colony, Georgia, founded

1754–1763 French and Indian War

Additional Resources

- Animal Trackers series by Tessa Paul (Crabtree, 1997) contains four titles that are written for children: *By Lakes and Rivers*, *By the Seashore*, *In Fields and Meadows*, and *In Woods and Forests*.

- *Animal Tracks: An Introduction to the Tracks and Signs of Familiar North American Species* by James Kavanagh (Waterford Press, 1997)

- *Cobblestone*, April 1993: "The Cultures of Pre-Columbian North America"

- *The Complete Tracker: Tracks, Signs, and Habits of North American Wildlife* by Len McDougall (Lyons Press, 1997)

- *Discover American Indian Ways: A Carnegie Activity Book* by Pamela Soeder (Roberts Rinehart, 1998)

- *The First Americans* by Joy Hakim (Oxford University Press Children's Books, 1999)

- *Food and Recipes of the Native Americans* by George Erdosh (Powerkids Press, 1998)

- *National Museum of the American Indian* **www.nmai.si.edu/** This Web site features exhibits, books, videos, events and activities, and links.

- *The Native American Look Book: Art and Activities from the Brooklyn Museum* by Missy Sullivan, Deborah Schwartz, Dawn Weiss, and Barbara Zaffran (New Press, 1996)

- *North American Indians* by Andrew Haslam (Two-Can Publishers, 2000)

- *Outdoor Action Animal Tracking Cards* **www.princeton.edu/~oa/nature/trackcard.shtml** This page, maintained by Princeton University, contains animal tracking cards that you can download and print from your computer.

- *Stokes' Guide to Animal Tracking and Behavior* by Donald and Lillian Stokes (Little, Brown, 1987)

- *The World of the American Indian* (National Geographic Society, 1994)

Great Gourds!

North American Indians discovered that they could attract birds to their crops by making houses for them out of hollowed-out gourds. The birds were beneficial to the Indians because they ate pests that might damage the crops. Purple martins became so accustomed to the man-made houses that, over time, nearly all the birds living east of the Rocky Mountains stopped making their homes in cliffs (their natural nesting sites) altogether. Today these birds rely on humans to provide their housing for them!

In addition to making birdhouses, Indians used gourds to create water dippers, rattles, and other types of containers.

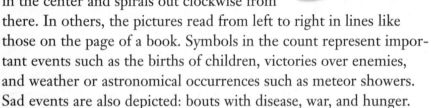

Winter Count

American Indians didn't have a written language but many of them "wrote" in pictures. The Plains Indians kept records of past events by drawing on buffalo hides. These records were called winter counts. The story told in some winter counts begins in the center and spirals out clockwise from there. In others, the pictures read from left to right in lines like those on the page of a book. Symbols in the count represent important events such as the births of children, victories over enemies, and weather or astronomical occurrences such as meteor showers. Sad events are also depicted: bouts with disease, war, and hunger.

Making a winter count will not only give students an opportunity to reflect on the important events in their lives but will also help them appreciate the Indians' use of symbols to tell a story.

What to Do

Explain what a winter count is and show students some examples of Indian picture writing found in reference books. *Make It Work! North American Indians* by Andrew Haslam (Two-Can Publishers, 2000) is one good resource. Then pass out copies of the reproducible instructions on page 9. Students can follow the directions to create their own winter counts.

If students have trouble coming up with ideas for their own winter counts, and if you've just started a new school year, suggest a fun twist on an old idea: They describe what they did over their summer vacations using symbols.

Once everyone is finished, display the counts and let students try to figure out what they say before the artist explains it to the group. Follow up with a brief discussion of which symbols are easiest to understand and why.

What You Need for Each Student:

- ♦ copy of the directions, page 9
- ♦ reference books
- ♦ paper grocery bag
- ♦ scrap paper
- ♦ pencil
- ♦ scissors
- ♦ colored pencils or markers

Give Me a Sign

Hundreds of North American Indian groups spoke more than 300 different languages. To communicate with other groups, they developed sign language not unlike that used by deaf people to communicate today.

Winter Count

What You Need:
♦ reference books
♦ paper grocery bag
♦ scrap paper
♦ pencil
♦ scissors
♦ colored pencils or markers

Directions

1. Cut apart a paper grocery bag to make a flat, oblong piece of paper and then cut out a hide shape from the paper, making it as large as possible.

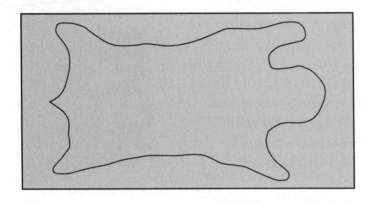

2. Think about what to include in the winter count. It can record important events in your whole life or just the past year.

3. After deciding what to include, list the events on a piece of paper. Next to each event, draw a picture, or symbol, that clearly represents the event. Keep the symbols simple. Try to make them easy to understand so that others can read your winter count.

4. Using colored pencils or markers, draw the symbols on the paper hide. Begin in the center of the hide and continue outward in a clockwise direction so that the oldest events are in the middle and the most recent are around the outside.

5. Can any of your classmates figure out the symbols that describe the events that are important to you?

6. See if you can read someone else's winter count.

Medicine Bag

The Pueblo Indians, like many Native Americans, believe that all things—from rocks and trees to wolves and people—possess a spirit. They collect small natural objects that are special to them in medicine bags that they wear close to their body. Medicine to North American Indians is not what we commonly think of today in terms of doctors or pills, but a spiritual power that protects a person. By collecting and keeping special objects in a medicine bag, the wearer harnesses the good spirit within the objects. That power helps him or her along the path of life.

Students can make medicine bags to hold precious objects of their own. After making the bags, encourage them to go on a "quest" as a North American Indian might, to find special things to place in the bag. Examples of items to choose include interesting rocks, small seeds or cones, seashells, even jewelry. Anything that has special meaning or speaks to the child in some way is fine.

What to Do

Provide students with copies of the reproducible directions on page 11, as well as the various materials needed to create their own medicine bags. Encourage them to use decorations like those used by the Pueblo Indians. Show some examples in books. Medicine bags usually are worn around the neck, but children can also tie them onto belt loops.

What You Need for Each Student:

- ♦ copy of the directions, page 11
- ♦ 8½-inch by 8-inch piece of tan felt
- ♦ scraps of other colored felt
- ♦ scissors
- ♦ glue
- ♦ yarn or raffia
- ♦ reference books
- ♦ small beads OPTIONAL
- ♦ fabric paint OPTIONAL
- ♦ colored markers OPTIONAL

False Faces and Helpful Spirits

To the Iroquois of New York, health care can be quite different from traditional European medicine. The Iroquois summon helpful spirits by wearing masks carved in the spirits' likenesses and offering tobacco and corn to them. The spirits have the power to cure the sick. The masks are called false faces and are carved from wood. The faces often have crooked noses, large eyes, and wide lips. Most also have long hair. The masks are very powerful and are even thought to be alive. When the healer puts on the mask and performs the ritual, the spirits come through him to heal the sick.

Medicine Bag

Directions

1. Fold the tan felt in half to make a shape that is 8½ inches long and 4 inches wide. Unfold the felt and run a line of glue 1½ inches from what will be the bottom edge of the bag and up the side, as shown. Refold the felt, lining up the edges. Then place the bag under a heavy book to press the sides together until the glue dries.

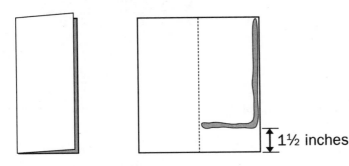

1½ inches

2. Cut fringes at the bottom of the bag, being careful not to cut into the glued "seam."

3. Fold the top edge down about ½ inch. Use scissors to cut small slits across the fold about 1 inch apart, as shown. Unfold the top edge and weave a 24-inch length of raffia or yarn drawstring through the slits. If you like, you can thread beads onto the string as well.

4. Cut out pieces of colored felt to glue to your bag as decoration. You can also use colored markers or fabric paint to draw designs on your bag. Allow the glue and paint time to dry completely.

5. Tie the string into a knot to wear the medicine bag around your neck, or tie it around a belt loop.

6. Begin your quest for special objects to place in the medicine bag.

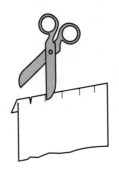

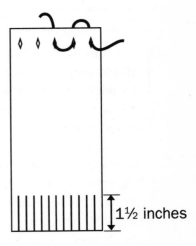

1½ inches

Bowl Game

This simple game is believed to have been played by many Indian groups across North America. Sometimes players wagered on the outcomes of the games. The playing pieces might have been carved from antler or bone, or made of plum or peach pits.

What to Do

1. Color in a wide stripe with the black marker on only one side of each of the pits or nut shells.

2. Give each player 20 counters. From the set of 20 counters, a player puts aside the number of points scored.

3. Place the pits into the bowl. Have the first player flip the pits into the air and try to catch them in the bowl. The player scores one point for each pit that lands stripe-side up in the bowl. There are no points awarded for pits that land outside the bowl, even if the stripe is showing.

4. The next player takes a turn, and so on.

5. The player who reaches 20 points (runs out of counters) first wins.

What You Need for Each Group of Four Students:

- shallow bowl or basket
- 6 peach or plum pits (washed and dried) or almonds in the shell
- black marker
- 80 toothpicks or dried beans for keeping score (20 for each player)

Lacrosse: America's Game

The game of lacrosse comes to us from the Eastern Woodland Indians, who played with wooden or hide-covered balls and netted sticks not unlike those used in the game today. Players could number from a few to hundreds. Sometimes Indian groups competed against each other in huge matches. The game was not only fast-paced and fun to watch, but it also helped condition and train warriors.

Learning Nature's Ways

Being able to survive in nature was crucial to Native Americans. They needed to know which types of plants they could eat or use in daily life and which ones were poisonous. Successful hunting required them to know the ways of animals. To learn and hone such skills, Indian boys played games. In many Native American groups, girls and boys were raised differently. Girls stayed home and helped their mothers and sisters with chores, while boys had more freedom to explore and play games. Since things have changed a lot over the years, both girls and boys can now have fun learning these skills.

What to Do

Take students outside in your schoolyard or nearby park and explain that they are going to play some nature games designed to teach them about the various plants and animals living around them.

What You Need for the Class:

- leaves of plants and trees from schoolyard or a park
- paper or plastic bag
- copies of animal tracks activity, page 15
- recorded animal calls (see page 14 for sources)
- plant and animal field guides
- paper and pencils

Looking at Leaves

1. Before class begins, go out in your schoolyard or a nearby park and collect a leaf from as many different trees and plants as you can find. (If you choose to visit a park, check first with the park ranger to help you avoid any rare or harmful plants or trees that may be growing there.) Put the leaves in a paper or plastic bag.

2. Show the group the leaves that you collected earlier. Students should sketch the leaves and make notes about their color, size, and any identifying characteristics. After everyone has finished, children in groups of four or five can try to find the trees and plants from which the leaves were taken. Then with the aid of field guides they should write down the name of each plant next to the appropriate sketches.

3. After students have located as many of the plants as possible, gather everyone together to discuss the identity of each leaf and the location of each plant. Are there any interesting features about the plants? Are any edible? Do any have medicinal properties?

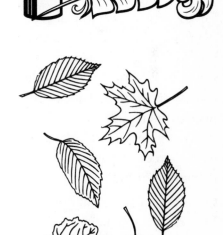

Listening to Animals

1. Explain to students that Native Americans not only recognized the calls of wild animals but also were able to imitate many of them. They sometimes used the calls to signal others while hunting or when they didn't want to be detected. You may be able to find recordings of animal sounds at your library. You can also sample bird calls at **http://birds.cornell.edu/sow/**, the Cornell Laboratory of Ornithology Web site. Hear sample bird, mammal, amphibian, and insect sounds from around the world at **www.bl.uk/collections/sound-archive/wildex.html**, the British Library's National Sound Archive Web site. Play recordings of several of the calls for the class. Have students guess what animals the calls belong to. Then reveal the answers.

2. Encourage kids to try to imitate the calls. Award the best callers with applause!

Identifying Animal Tracks

1. Give a copy of the animal tracks activity on page 15 to each student and divide the class into groups of four or five. Tell them that as young Indians they need to identify some recent tracks found in the mud. Students should first guess which animals correspond with the tracks. As a class, encourage them to discuss the reasons that led them to their answers. Then have them use animal field guides to check their guesses (see suggested resources on page 7). Go over the correct answers after everyone has finished.

2. Observe actual animal tracks by setting up a "track catcher." First clear a soil patch of plants, leaves, and so forth. Then rake it smooth. The soil should be soft enough that impressions can be made in it. Muddy soil works well if it's not too wet. It's best to choose an area where animals are likely to be, such as near a stream or beneath a bird feeder. Wait until the next morning to check for signs of visitors. Use field guides to identify any tracks you find.

Answers 1. gray squirrel **2.** rabbit **3.** owl **4.** fox **5.** bear **6.** cat **7.** duck **8.** deer **9.** opossum **10.** crow **11.** pigeon **12.** mouse

Identifying Animal Tracks

Look at the animal tracks below. What animals could have made the tracks?
Write your idea in each box. Be ready to discuss any clues that led to your answers.

1.	2.	3.

4.	5.	6.

7.	8.	9.

10.	11.	12.

Fry Bread

Indians in the Southwest, such as the Pueblo, grew corn and made a flat bread from its flour called fry bread. The bread could be eaten plain, or topped with honey, jam, or beans. If you have trouble finding corn flour, substitute all-purpose flour.

Note: Supervise children carefully around the hot plate and skillet. Do not allow children to put the dough in the skillet, turn it, or remove it. Handle that part yourself.

What to Do

1. Write the list of recipe ingredients and student directions below on the chalkboard. Your students can be responsible for preparing the fry bread dough. Once the dough is prepared, you can follow steps 2–5 below to cook it for the class.

2. Pour vegetable oil in the skillet to a depth of 1 inch. Slowly heat the oil on low.

3. When the oil is hot, use a fork to put a dough patty into the skillet. Be very careful not to get burned or let the hot oil splash onto your skin. Cook the bread on one side until it is golden brown (about 2–3 minutes). Turn the bread over and cook the other side for about 2 minutes.

4. Remove the bread and place it on paper towels to drain.

5. Fry the remaining pieces of dough, adding oil to the skillet as needed. Then enjoy the bread while it's warm!

Steps for Students

1. Mix together the flour, baking powder, and salt in a large bowl.

2. In a small bowl, stir together the dried milk, water, and vegetable oil.

3. Pour this liquid over the dry ingredients and stir until the dough is smooth (1 or 2 minutes). Add 1 tablespoon of flour if the dough is too soft or 1 teaspoon of water if it is too crumbly.

4. Coat your hands with flour and knead the dough in the bowl for about 30 seconds. Cover it with a cloth and let the dough sit for 10 minutes.

5. Shape the dough into balls about the size of a lime. Place the balls on waxed paper. Flatten each dough ball to form a patty about ¼ inch thick.

What You Need to Make One Batch of Bread (8 pieces):

- electric hot plate
- large skillet
- vegetable oil for frying
- large and small mixing bowls
- measuring cups and spoons
- spoon
- cloth towel
- fork
- paper towels
- waxed paper

Recipe Ingredients:

- 2½ cups corn or all-purpose flour
- 1½ tablespoons baking powder
- 1 teaspoon salt
- 1 tablespoon dried skimmed milk or soy milk powder
- ¾ cup warm water
- 1 tablespoon vegetable oil
- jelly or honey for bread topping

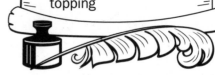

Colonial America: Settlement and Revolution

After Europeans reached the Americas, a race to claim land and colonize the "New World" began. Britain, France, and Spain each staked territories. France claimed lands stretching from Canada south to the Gulf of Mexico. Spain held lands from California through Texas and Mexico. Britain's 13 colonies ranged along the Atlantic Coast from Massachusetts to Georgia. Colonizing a new land was difficult, and many people died in the attempt. But the hope of finding gold or other riches or the chance of enjoying religious freedom drew thousands of people to the Americas. Africans were brought to the colonies and sold as slaves as early as 1619.

Soon villages, towns, and farms were established in all 13 British colonies. Most colonies had a governor who was appointed by the king of England. Disagreements over colonists' rights and political ideologies led to growing unrest in America. Britain's tax on tea spurred colonists in the so-called Boston Tea Party to board British ships in Boston Harbor and dump 342 chests of tea into the ocean. In 1774, colonists held the First Continental Congress. Delegates from every colony except Georgia met to express their displeasure with unfair British rule. By the next year, the situation had grown serious. Although no colonists were elected to the British Parliament, that governing body passed taxes levied in America. "Taxation without representation" was one of the main catalysts for the American Revolution, which began in 1775. The Second Continental Congress met a month later and formed the Continental Army, led by George Washington, to defend the colonies. On July 4, 1776, the Declaration of Independence was signed, but it would be another seven years before the Revolution would officially end, finally giving the colonies their freedom.

The colonies then had to set up a government. The Articles of Confederation, the first constitution, allowed for a very limited national government. State governments had more power than the national government under the articles. When it was realized that a stronger central government was needed—to raise and maintain a national army and print a common currency, for example—delegates from the states met to draft a new constitution. It was ratified by 1788, and the Bill of Rights, or first ten amendments to the Constitution, were added three years later. The Constitution, which outlined the system of government that we have today, called for a national president to be elected by the people.

But the young United States still had to prove itself to other countries. The War of 1812 resulted from interference by Britain and France in American affairs. When the United States prevailed in the war and later issued the Monroe Doctrine, which forbade additional European colonies in the Americas and separated American and European governments, its sovereignty as a nation was solidified.

Time Line

1773 Boston Tea Party

1774 First Continental Congress

1775 Battles of Lexington and Concord

1776 Declaration of Independence completed

1781 Articles of Confederation adopted

1783 Treaty of Paris ends the Revolutionary War

1788 U.S. Constitution ratified

1789 George Washington becomes first U.S. president

1812 War of 1812 with Britain

1823 Monroe Doctrine

Additional Resources

- *America's Homepage*
  www.pilgrims.net/plymouth
  A Web site about the Plymouth colony.

- *And Then What Happened, Paul Revere?* by Jean Fritz (Paperstar, 1996)

- *Archiving Early America*
  www.earlyamerica.com
  This Web site displays original newspapers, maps, and writings from eighteenth-century America.

- *Cobblestone,* September 1983: "Patriotic Tales of the American Revolution"

- *Cobblestone,* June 1990: "Colonial Craftsmen"

- *Colonial Crafts* by Bobbie Kalman (Crabtree, 1992)

- *Colonial Williamsburg*
  www.history.org
  This Web site contains information about the historic community and numerous educational resources, including lesson plans, books and videos, and electronic field trips.

- *Felicity's Cook Book* by Jodi Evert (Pleasant Company Publications, 1994)

- *Felicity's Craft Book* by Jodi Evert (Pleasant Company Publications, 1994)

- *Food and Recipes of the Pilgrims, Food and Recipes of the Revolutionary War,* and *Food and Recipes of the Thirteen Colonies* by George Erdosh (Powerkids Press, 1998)

- *The Paul Revere House*
  www.paulreverehouse.org
  This Boston landmark maintains a Web site with biographical information on Revere as well as details of his ride on April 18, 1775. The map accompanying information on the midnight ride is especially helpful.

- *ReadAloud Plays: Revolutionary War* by Dallas Murphy (Scholastic, 2000) contains five exciting fact-based plays, writing prompts, discussion questions, and creative activity ideas.

- *The Revolutionaries* edited by Russell B. Adams Jr. (Time-Life, 1996) contains a detailed account of Revere's ride.

- *What Was the Name of Paul Revere's Horse? Twenty Questions About Paul Revere, Asked and Answered* by Patrick M. Leehey (Paul Revere Memorial Association, 1997)

Was There Any Mail at the Inn?

Taverns and inns served as the first post offices in the early days of the colonies. By the late 1600s, the British monarch appointed postmasters, the most famous of them being Benjamin Franklin, who served for more than 20 years. In 1781, the Articles of Confederation gave the United States the power to establish a national post office. Finally in 1847, the United States issued its first postage stamps.

Fabric Dyeing

Early American colonists had to make just about everything they needed, from clothing and candles to paper and ink. Making clothing was a long process. Colonists spun thread out of flax and wool. After spinning, the thread was woven into cloth that could be turned into whatever the family needed. Of course the clothes would all be the same color unless the fibers were dyed. Nature supplied the colors for the dyes. Pokeberries and wild cherries made pink dye, lily of the valley and bayberry leaves made green, and goldenrod flowers and onion skins made yellow. After you dye the fabric, students can use it for the cat pincushion in the next chapter.

What You Need:
- hot plate
- 1-gallon pot
- water
- long-handled spoon
- alum
- cream of tartar
- white cotton cloth—about 12 inches square for each student (recycle old T-shirts, cloth handkerchiefs, etc.)
- 1 bag of yellow onions—enough to gather a handful of yellow onion skins
- basin

What to Do

1. Make sure the cotton cloth is clean. If it is new, wash it before dyeing.

2. Fill the pot three-quarters full with water. Add 1 tablespoon alum and 3 tablespoons cream of tartar and stir. The alum and cream of tartar (both found in the spice section of grocery stores) act as a mordant, which makes the cotton absorb more of the dye. Without the mordant, the fabric will not assume a rich color. Add the fabric pieces and simmer the pot over low heat for 20 to 30 minutes. The water should cover the fabric completely. You may need additional pots if you have a large group. For both soaking and dyeing, the fabric pieces should move freely through the water without bunching up.

3. Remove the fabric from the mordant and wring it out once it's cool enough to handle. Empty the mordant mixture, wash the pot, and fill it with clean water. Simmer over low heat.

4. Invite students to remove the dry outer skins from a bag of onions.

5. Place the onion skins into the pot of water, add the fabric pieces, and simmer for 15 to 20 minutes, stirring occasionally. The longer you leave the fabric in the dye, the deeper the yellow color will be. Stirring also helps evenly distribute the dye.

6. Carefully remove the fabric from the dye and put it in a basin of cool water to rinse. Rinse until the water is clear. Then wring out the fabric and hang it up to dry.

Graceful Toy

Although playing graces was meant to help young girls be elegant, it's fun for boys as well.

What to Do

1. If you need to, saw the dowels in half. Do not allow students to use the saw, but do it for them.

2. Working over sheets of newspaper, lightly sand the dowels and hoop so there are no rough edges or splinters.

3. Write the student directions below on the chalkboard.

Steps for Students

1. Paint the hoop and sticks and let them dry completely.

2. Tie the ribbons around the hoop.

3. To play the game, toss the hoop back and forth with a partner, touching it only with the sticks. The object is never to let the hoop touch the ground. If you master tossing one hoop, try using two.

What You Need for Each Student Pair:

- ◆ wooden hoop about 9 inches in diameter (inside embroidery hoop works well)
- ◆ 2 sticks about 18 inches long and ¼ inch wide (¼-inch dowels cut in half work well)
- ◆ fine sandpaper
- ◆ acrylic paint
- ◆ paintbrushes
- ◆ water
- ◆ colored ribbons about 30 inches long
- ◆ scissors
- ◆ newspapers

Goosey Game

Colonial children played board games just as girls and boys do today. But instead of Monopoly or Battleship, they played games such as Nine-Men's Morris or Goose. Like the Game of Life, the goal of Goose is to reach the end of a path, and along the way lurk all sorts of spaces that can trip up each player.

What to Do

1. Provide students with copies of the reproducible game board on pages 22–23, as well as the various materials needed to create their own games.

2. To assemble the game board, have students cut along the solid line at the right side of page 22. Match the two sides of the game board and then tape together. To make the board more durable, glue it to a sheet of thin cardboard.

3. Read the Goosey Game directions on page 22.

What You Need for Each Group of Four Students:

- copy of the game board, pages 22–23
- 2 number cubes
- 4 place markers, such as buttons or counters
- tape
- thin cardboard
- glue
- scissors

This Sub's a Turtle

The first American submarine used in war was the *Turtle*, a one-man sub deployed during the Revolution to deliver a bomb to an enemy ship. The wooden sub wasn't much larger than the person stationed inside. Its name probably came from its oblong, turtle-shell shape. The vessel was operated by hand-cranking propellers, and submerged when water was allowed to flood the lower portion of the craft. The submarine returned to the surface by pumping out the water again. The *Turtle* saw action only once. When it failed to attach its bomb to the hull of the HMS *Eagle*, it was mothballed.

Goosey Game

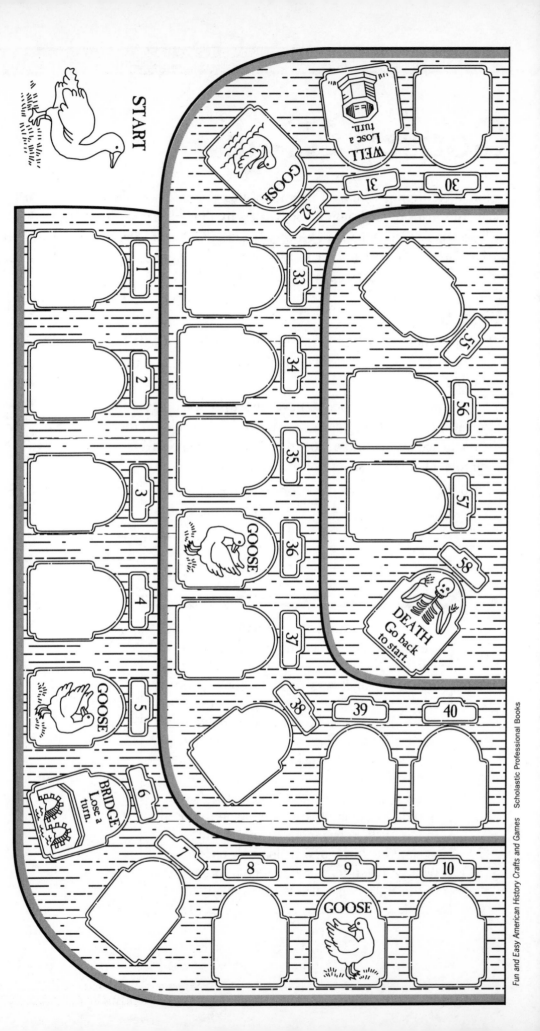

START

In turn, players roll the number cubes and move their markers that number of spaces on the board.

◆ If a player lands on a space with instructions, the player must follow them.

◆ If a player lands on a GOOSE space, the player moves again the same number of spaces. If this extra move lands the player on another GOOSE, the player again moves the same number of spaces forward.

The first person to reach "The End" in the center wins. (The roll to reach the center space must be exact.)

All players begin at the space marked "start." Roll the number cubes to see who goes first, then take turns after that.

1 2 3 4 5 6 7 8 9 10

33 34 35 36 37 38 39 40

GOOSE

BRIDGE
Lose a turn.

GOOSE

55 56 57 58

DEATH
Go back to start.

30 31 32

WELL
Lose a turn.

GOOSE

Fun and Easy American History Crafts and Games   Scholastic Professional Books

29 28 27 GOOSE 26 25 24

54 GOOSE 53 PRISON Lose a turn. 52 51 50 GOOSE 23 GOOSE 22

63 THE END 62 49 21

59 60 61 48 20

GOOSE 47 19 TAVERN Lose a turn.

46 18 GOOSE

41 GOOSE 42 MAZE Go back to square 20. 43 44 45 GOOSE 17

11 12 13 14 GOOSE 15 16

Put Your John Hancock Here

John Hancock, proud to attach his name to the Declaration of Independence, signed in huge, bold strokes—the most prominent signature on the document. To this day, putting your John Hancock on something means to sign it.

What to Do

Explain to students that a signature, usually written in script, is a special way of signing one's own name. Often, people use signatures to show that they agree with something that is written. Ask students to imagine that they are going to sign a very important document, such as the Declaration of Independence. Encourage them to create and practice their own special signature.

What You Need for Each Student:
- copy of the activity below
- pen, pencils, or markers

Name _____

Put Your John Hancock Here

One of the most famous signatures in American history is that of John Hancock. When he was president of the Second Continental Congress, he proudly attached his name to the Declaration of Independence. He signed in huge, bold strokes—large enough so that King George wouldn't need his spectacles to read it! To this day putting your John Hancock on something means to sign it.

In the spaces below, create and practice your own special signature.

The Real Revere

Henry Wadsworth Longfellow's "Paul Revere's Ride" helped make the Massachusetts silversmith famous. But the 1860 poem paints a mythical portrait of the ride. Revere was not the only messenger that night sent to Lexington to warn of the invading British army, which had been ordered not only to seize a weapons supply that the Patriots had gathered at Concord but also to arrest Revolutionary leaders Samuel Adams and John Hancock. In fact Revere was captured by a British patrol. Instead, fellow rider Samuel Prescott escaped and continued to Concord to warn the people of the coming attack. Nevertheless, Revere was a great patriot who participated in the Boston Tea Party and rode as a courier between Philadelphia and New York many times for the cause of independence. Although Revere did not complete his journey on April 19, 1775, he and his fellow riders managed to warn Adams and Hancock to flee. Along the way, they alerted many colonists who were ready to fight when the redcoats arrived.

Longfellow also distorted the lantern signal "one, if by land, and two, if by sea." The signals from the steeple of Boston's Old North Church were used to indicate the method of the invasion, but Revere arranged them the week before, and they had nothing to do with his famous ride. Instead, another courier was dispatched upon the lantern signal but was stopped almost immediately by British troops.

While Longfellow's poem is certainly more compelling as it's written, if it had been completely accurate, we might not remember Revere today!

What to Do

1. Hand out copies of "Paul Revere's Ride" to the group and read it aloud. Discuss the poem and what students know about Paul Revere and his famous ride. Help children with words and references that they may not understand.

What You Need for Each Student:
- ♦ copy of "Paul Revere's Ride," pages 26–27
- ♦ paper and pen
- ♦ research materials

2. Divide the class into small groups and ask them to go through the poem, picking out details that seem to relate the facts of Revere's ride. Have them write a brief summary of the ride as Longfellow describes it.

3. Ask students to research the actual ride on the night of April 18–19, 1775. They can use encyclopedias, the Internet, and other reference materials, including those suggested on page 18. After completing their research, they should write a revised summary of Revere's ride based on the facts as historians know them. Encourage students to make a time line showing Revere's progress throughout the evening.

4. Once finished, ask students to compare Longfellow's version to the historical one. Help them answer these questions:
   - ♦ Why does the poem tell a different story? *(It is a work of art and not a historical document. Longfellow was inspired by the story of Revere and wrote about it from his own imagination.)*
   - ♦ If Longfellow had stuck to the facts in his poem, would it be as enjoyable? *(Probably not. The real story is not as entertaining as the one created in the poem.)*
   - ♦ Is it okay for a poet or writer to embellish or exaggerate when writing a poem or story?

5. Encourage students to write new verses to "Paul Revere's Ride" that tell the true story as they've pieced together from their research. Share the results with the group.

6. As an extension, students can dig a bit deeper into the life of Paul Revere and prepare brief biographies of this American patriot.

Paul Revere's Ride

Henry Wadsworth Longfellow

Listen my children, and you shall hear
Of the midnight ride of Paul Revere,
On the eighteenth of April, in seventy-five;
Hardly a man is now alive
Who remembers that famous day and year.

He said to his friend, "If the British march
By land or sea from the town tonight,
Hang a lantern aloft in the belfry arch
Of the North Church tower as a signal light,—
One, if by land, and two, if by sea;
And I on the opposite shore will be,
Ready to ride and spread the alarm
Through every Middlesex village and farm,
For the country folk to be up and to arm."

Then he said, "Good-night!" and with muffled oar
Silently rowed to the Charlestown shore.
Just as the moon rose over the bay,
Where swinging wide at her moorings lay
The *Somerset*, British man-of-war;
A phantom ship, with each mast and spar
Across the moon like a prison bar,
And a huge black hulk, that was magnified
By its own reflection in the tide.

Meanwhile, his friend, through alley and street,
Wanders and watches with eager ears,
Till in the silence around him he hears
The muster of men at the barrack door,
The sound of arms, and the tramp of feet,
And the measured tread of the grenadiers,
Marching down to their boats on the shore.

Then he climbed the tower of the Old North Church,
By the wooden stairs, with stealthy tread,
To the belfry-chamber overhead,
And startled the pigeons from their perch
On the somber rafters, that round him made
Masses and moving shapes of shade,—
By the trembling ladder, steep and tall,
To the highest window in the wall,

Where he paused to listen and look down
A moment on the roofs of the town,
And the moonlight flowing over all.

Beneath, in the churchyard, lay the dead,
In their night-encampment on the hill,
Wrapped in silence so deep and still
That he could hear, like a sentinel's tread,
The watchful night-wind, as it went
Creeping along from tent to tent,
And seemed to whisper, "All is well!"
A moment only he feels the spell
Of the place and the hour, and the
    secret dread
Of the lonely belfry and the dead;
For suddenly all his thoughts are bent
On a shadowy something far away,
Where the river widens to meet the bay,—
A line of black that bends and floats
On the rising tide, like a bridge of boats.

Meanwhile, impatient to mount and ride,
Booted and spurred, with a heavy stride
On the opposite shore walked Paul Revere.
Now he patted his horse's side,
Now he gazed at the landscape far
    and near,
Then, impetuous, stamped the earth,
And turned and tightened his saddle-girth;
But mostly he watched with eager search
The belfry-tower of the Old North Church,
As it rose above the graves on the hill,
Lonely and spectral and somber and still.

And lo! as he looks, on the belfry's height
A glimmer, and then a gleam of light!
He springs to the saddle, the bridle he
    turns,
But lingers and gazes, till full on his sight
A second lamp in the belfry burns!

Paul Revere's Ride (continued)

A hurry of hoofs in a village street,
A shape in the moonlight, a bulk in the dark,
And beneath, from the pebbles, in passing,
  a spark
Struck out by a steed flying fearless and fleet:
That was all! And yet, through the gloom and
  the light
The fate of a nation was riding that night;
And the spark struck out by that steed, in
  his flight,
Kindled the land into flame with its heat.

He has left the village and mounted the steep,
And beneath him, tranquil and broad and deep,
Is the Mystic, meeting the ocean tides;
And under the alders that skirt its edge,
Now soft on the sand, now loud on the ledge,
Is heard the tramp of his steed as he rides.

It was twelve by the village clock,
When he crossed the bridge into Medford town.
He heard the crowing of the cock,
And the barking of the farmer's dog,
And felt the damp of the river fog
That rises after the sun goes down.

It was one by the village clock,
When he galloped into Lexington.
He saw the gilded weathercock
Swing in the moonlight as he passed.
And the meeting-house windows, blank
  and bare,
Gaze at him with a spectral glare,
As if they already stood aghast
At the bloody work they would look upon.

It was two by the village clock,
When he came to the bridge in Concord town.
He heard the bleating of the flock,
And the twitter of birds among the trees,
And felt the breath of the morning breeze
Blowing over the meadows brown.
And one was safe and asleep in his bed
Who at the bridge would be first to fall,
Who that day would be lying dead,
Pierced by a British musket-ball.

You know the rest. In all the books you
  have read,
How the British Regulars fired and fled,—
How the farmers gave them ball for ball,
From behind each fence and farm-yard wall,
Chasing the red-coats down the lane,
Then crossing the fields to emerge again
Under the trees at the turn of the road,
And only pausing to fire and load.

So through the night rode Paul Revere;
And so through the night went his cry of alarm
To every Middlesex village and farm,—
A cry of defiance and not of fear,
A voice in the darkness, a knock at the door,
And a word that shall echo forevermore!
For, borne on the night-wind of the Past,
Through all our history, to the last,
In the hour of darkness and peril and need,
The people will waken and listen to hear
The hurrying hoof-beats of that steed,
  and the midnight message of Paul Revere.

Fun and Easy American History Crafts and Games   Scholastic Professional Books

Johnny Cakes

"Johny cakes" (johnny cakes) were included in a cookbook by Amelia Simmons published in 1796. They are similar to pancakes but are made with cornmeal, which the colonists incorporated into their diet following the example of Native Americans. Unlike pancakes, johnny cakes were eaten anytime and may have been served with honey, molasses, beans, or meat.

What to Do

1. Heat the milk and butter in a saucepan until they boil. Stir while heating to be sure the milk doesn't scald.

2. While the milk and butter heat, mix the cornmeal, salt, and molasses in a large bowl.

3. Pour the boiling milk and butter into the dry ingredients and stir until the batter is well mixed.

4. Grease the skillet with butter and heat over medium-low heat.

5. Pour batter into the skillet, about ⅓ cup at a time, to make the cakes. Try to keep the batter from one cake from running into the others.

6. Fry about 4 minutes, or until the cakes are brown on the bottom. Then flip the cakes and cook on the other side for about 1 minute more.

7. Serve the finished cakes with honey, syrup, preserves, or butter (recipe for homemade butter found on page 40).

What You Need to Make 8 Cakes:
- hot plate
- large bowl
- spoon
- measuring cups and spoons
- small saucepan
- skillet
- spatula

Recipe Ingredients:
- 1 cup milk
- 2 tablespoons butter
- 1 cup cornmeal
- ½ teaspoon salt
- 2 tablespoons molasses
- butter to grease skillet
- honey, syrup, butter, or preserves as toppings

An Illuminating Time
During the holidays, the windows of many homes twinkle with the light of candles. You may not know that this custom dates back to colonial times. For very special occasions such as Christmas Eve, homeowners placed lighted candles in their windows. This tradition came to be known as an illumination. In historic Williamsburg, Virginia, today, you can still see an illumination every Christmas season.

Pioneers: Moving West

After the United States gained its freedom from Britain, Americans steadily began to move into former British territories that were east of the Mississippi River. The United States now stretched from present-day Maine to the border of Florida and west to the Mississippi as far north as Canada. Then in 1803 the size of the country doubled with the Louisiana Purchase. With the support of President Thomas Jefferson, Secretary of State James Madison arranged to buy from France all land west of the Mississippi River to the Rocky Mountains.

People began moving west in wagons, loaded with all their belongings and supplies, along several trails that ultimately led thousands to their new homes. The Cumberland, Oregon, Santa Fe, and California trails were major routes. For safety, pioneers often traveled in groups called wagon trains. The trip was difficult. Harsh weather, accidents, and illness plagued the pioneers. Native Americans resented the settlers claiming their lands and sometimes fought to preserve their home and their way of life. But the overwhelming number of settlers and government-sponsored relocations eventually pushed Native Americans off their lands and onto reservations.

The United States acquired even more land after Texas won its independence from Mexico and eventually became a U.S. state. The dispute over Texas led to the Mexican War (1846–1848). According to the peace treaty, which was signed in 1848, the United States gained from Mexico all of present-day California, Nevada, Utah, Arizona, and parts of New Mexico, Colorado, and Wyoming. By 1853, the United States held all the land that makes up the lower 48 states today. With the discovery of gold in California and the Homestead Act of 1862, which gave land to any settler willing to farm it for five years, settlement of the western United States was assured.

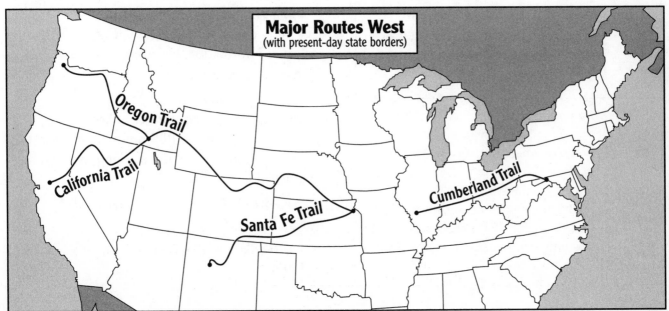

Major Routes West
(with present-day state borders)

Oregon Trail

California Trail

Santa Fe Trail

Cumberland Trail

Time Line

1803 United States buys Louisiana Territory from France

1805 Explorers Meriwether Lewis and William Clark reach the Pacific Ocean

1821 Mexico wins independence from Spain

1830 Indian Removal Act passes, enabling the United States to resettle Native Americans

1845 United States acquires Texas

1846–1848 Mexican War

1849 Height of the California Gold Rush

1862 Homestead Act passed

1876 Cheyenne and Sioux defeat General George Custer's army at Little Big Horn

1890 U.S. troops kill Sioux who had already surrendered at Wounded Knee, South Dakota

Additional Resources

♦ *Cobblestone*, September 1980: "Lewis and Clark"

♦ *Cobblestone*, December 1981: "The Oregon Trail"

♦ *Exploring the West from Monticello*
www.lib.virginia.edu/exhibits/lewis_clark/home.html
This site features maps from before and after Lewis and Clark's western exploration.

♦ *Food and Recipes of the Westward Expansion* by George Erdosh (Powerkids Press, 1998)

♦ *Home Crafts* by Bobbie Kalman (Crabtree, 1993)

♦ *Josefina's Cook Book* by Tamara England (Pleasant Company Publications, 1998)

♦ *Josefina's Craft Book* by Tamara England (Pleasant Company Publications, 1998)

♦ *Kirsten's Cook Book* by Jodi Evert (Pleasant Company Publications, 1994)

♦ *Kirsten's Craft Book* by Jodi Evert (Pleasant Company Publications, 1994)

♦ *Lewis and Clark* by Bonnie Sachatello-Sawyer (Scholastic, 1997) is an activity guide and poster for grades 4–8.

♦ *Lewis and Clark: The Journey of the Corps of Discovery*
www.pbs.org/lewisandclark
This companion to the PBS program features lots of information, classroom resources, and an interactive journey.

♦ *The Oregon Trail*
www.isu.edu/~trinmich/Oregontrail.html
A companion to the PBS program, this site features information on the trail and those who traveled it.

♦ *Pioneer Crafts* by Barbara Greenwood (Kids Can Press, 1997)

♦ *The Wagon Train* by Bobbie Kalman (Crabtree, 1999)

Twirling the Plate Game

This simple game could be played in any household, from a covered wagon to a homesteader's kitchen.

What to Do

1. Stand in a circle around a table that is larger than a desk but not so large that students can't reach across it.

2. One player sets the plate on its edge and spins it in the center of the table. The spinner calls out the name of one of the other players. That child must catch the plate before it stops spinning.

3. If the child catches the plate successfully, he or she then spins it and calls on another player, and so on. If a player fails to catch the plate, he or she doesn't get to spin but must pass the plate on to the player who spun before.

What You Need for Each Group of Four or Five Students:

- ◆ table
- ◆ nonbreakable plate or saucer

Watch for Flying Buffalo Chips!

In *Fantastic Facts About the Oregon Trail* (Boettcher/Trinklein, 1999), author Michael Trinklein says that pioneer children crossing the Great Plains found a way to amuse themselves with buffalo chips! Herds of buffalo roamed the plains and left behind lots of dung chips, which dried up to form round disks that children threw like Frisbees. But many more of the chips ended up in the pioneers' campfires. Can you imagine cooking over a dung fire?

Loosey Goosey Toy

Frontier children played with toys that either they made themselves or that an adult created for them. With scraps of wood, a parent or local woodworker might have crafted a toy like this one. You can construct it out of materials easy to find in the classroom or at a craft store.

What to Do

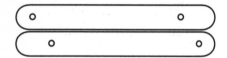

Make holes that are offset.

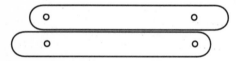

Line up holes to attach geese.

To prepare the craft sticks for your students, place them flat on a table or other surface protected by a pad of newspaper. Use the pointed end of scissors or an awl to make small holes in the craft sticks, as shown. To prevent the sticks from splitting, avoid making the holes too close to the sticks' ends. The holes need to be just large enough for a paper fastener to pass through. Be careful not to damage the table or other surface with the scissors.

Pass out copies of the directions and geese figures (page 33) and the other materials.

What You Need for Each Student:
- ◆ copy of the geese figures and directions, page 33
- ◆ thin cardboard
- ◆ glue
- ◆ colored pencils or markers
- ◆ scissors
- ◆ awl (for teacher use only)
- ◆ newspapers
- ◆ 2 large craft sticks
- ◆ 4 paper fasteners

Loosey Goosey Toy

What You Need:
- ♦ geese figures, below
- ♦ thin cardboard
- ♦ glue
- ♦ colored pencils or markers
- ♦ scissors
- ♦ 2 large craft sticks
- ♦ 4 paper fasteners

Directions

1. Color the geese. Then glue them to a thin piece of cardboard. Let dry and cut out around the solid lines.

2. Make small holes in the geese as indicated by the dots. Push paper fasteners through the holes on one goose and then through the holes in the pair of sticks and open the prongs to keep them in place. Do the same for the other goose, attaching it through the holes on the other end of the sticks.

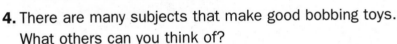

3. Hold the top stick with one hand and the bottom stick with the other. Pull the sticks apart and push them back together to see the geese bob back and forth.

4. There are many subjects that make good bobbing toys. What others can you think of?

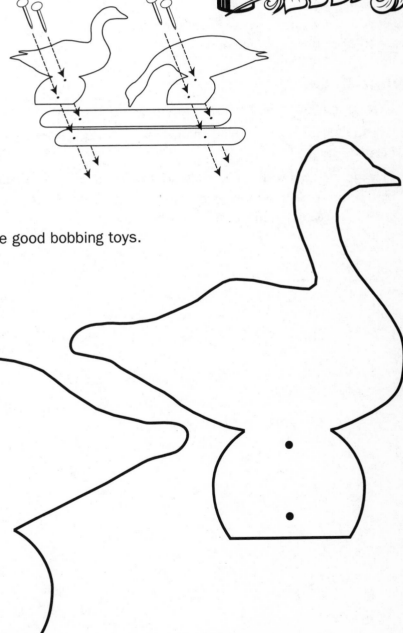

Cat Pincushion

Sewing was an important skill, especially for pioneer women and girls. Since there were no sewing machines, everything had to be mended and sewn by hand. At a young age, girls began learning to sew. Perhaps you've seen samplers made by young seamstresses. Not just for sewing practice, samplers often featured the alphabet, numbers, or verses that little girls needed to learn.

Making the cat pincushion helps both girls and boys practice sewing. After they're done, they'll have a handy place to store their pins and needles!

What to Do

1. Explain how important learning to sew was to the pioneers.

2. Ask students to share their ideas of the kinds of things pioneers needed to sew.

3. Provide students with copies of the reproducible directions and pattern on page 35, as well as the various materials needed to create their own cat pincushions.

What You Need for Each Student:

- ◆ copy of the directions, page 35
- ◆ 12-inch square of cotton fabric (the dyed fabric from page 19 is ideal)
- ◆ straight pins
- ◆ scissors
- ◆ matching thread
- ◆ needle
- ◆ markers
- ◆ cotton balls or fiberfill stuffing

Cat Pincushion

What You Need:
- 12-inch square of cotton fabric
- straight pins
- scissors
- matching thread
- needle
- markers
- cotton balls or fiberfill stuffing

Directions

1. Fold the fabric square in half, keeping the edges together.

2. Use a few straight pins to attach the pattern to the fabric, being sure to pin through both layers.

3. Cut out around the pattern, going through both layers of fabric at the same time. Remove the pins and the pattern.

4. On a piece of the cut-out fabric, use markers to draw in the cat's features.

5. Put the two pieces of fabric together so that the outside of the pincushion (the side with the drawn-in features) is on the inside and the edges align perfectly. Pin the pieces together.

6. Thread the needle and tie a knot at the end. Sew the pieces together, close to the edges, using a whipstitch, as shown. Begin sewing at the tip of the cat's tail and continue around the cat until you come to within an inch of where you started.

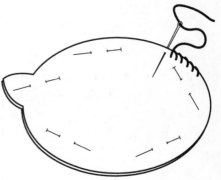

7. Remove the pins and turn the pincushion right side out. You may need to poke the eraser end of a pencil inside to help push the cat's ear right side out.

8. Stuff the pincushion with cotton balls or fiberfill stuffing until it's firm and plump.

9. Turn the rough edges of the fabric inside so they don't poke out, and continue whipstitching on the outside to close up the hole. Tie a knot after the last stitch and clip off any leftover thread.

Classroom Cartographers

When the United States bought the Louisiana Territory, few of its people knew what this vast tract of land was like. President Thomas Jefferson sent explorers Meriwether Lewis and William Clark to find out as much as possible about the new territory. But first the men needed to learn all they could about cartography, or mapmaking. They brought back information about the plants, animals, and geographic features they found, which helped create updated maps. Such maps, and subsequent ones made as settlers moved farther and farther west, were invaluable tools in the expansion of the United States. The activity that follows helps students appreciate the importance of maps.

What to Do

1. Students will gain an appreciation of maps when they have to locate something, first without the aid of a map and then with it. But before they begin, give them a historical perspective. Using books or the Exploring the West from Monticello Web site at **www.lib.virginia.edu/exhibits/lewis_clark/home.html**, show students pictures of maps made of the western United States before and after the Lewis and Clark expedition. If you look at a 1795 map by Aaron Arrowsmith, you can see that there is scarcely any detail past the Missouri River. But Lewis and Clark traveled to the Pacific, learning that there was no Northwest Passage (a water route to the Pacific) and amassing a great deal of information about the land along the way. Their trip helped fill in some of the gaps from the previous map.

2. Provide students with the maps on pages 38–39. Give students an opportunity to compare the two maps. Invite them to line up the images, holding them up to the light to discover the state or territory they would live in if the United States remained the way it was during Lewis and Clark's day. Encourage students to share their observations in a whole-class discussion.

3. Show students some modern maps and the kinds of information they show: roads, cities and towns, land use, and elevation.

4. Take the class outside to your schoolyard or to a nearby park. Assign a team of two students to find a landmark such as a specific tree or other feature that you have already picked out. Tell them where to look without being too specific. Begin timing the students when they set off to find the landmark and stop the

What You Need for the Class:
- ♦ copies of the maps, pages 38–39
- ♦ examples of maps
- ♦ stopwatch
- ♦ paper
- ♦ yardsticks
- ♦ string
- ♦ rulers
- ♦ colored markers
- ♦ directional compasses

watch when they return. The students should not reveal the location of the landmark to the rest of the class, only to you so that you can verify their success.

5. Have the two students draw a simple map, showing the location of the item they found. Have them include landmarks, distances, direction, and so forth.

6. Give the map to another pair of students and set them off to find the object, again using a stopwatch. With the help of the map, they should be able to find the item much more quickly.

7. Involve everyone by having groups of three or four students make their own maps of the area. Encourage them to use compasses to locate direction. They can measure distance in paces or with the help of string and yardsticks. Their maps should include major features, compass points, a scale, and any other pertinent information.

8. Once the students have completed the maps, compare them. Which are the easiest to read and why?

Guidance Worth Much More Than a Dollar

Sacajewea was a Shoshone native who had married a French Canadian assigned to Lewis and Clark's expedition. With her baby son riding on her back, Sacajewea led the explorers from present-day North Dakota to the Pacific Ocean and back. She acted as an interpreter, guide, and ambassador to the native people living along the way, who in turn helped the party by giving them supplies and information about the terrain. Because of her invaluable service, the United States honored Sacajewea by minting a one-dollar coin in her likeness in the year 2000.

The Journey of Lewis and Clark, 1804–1806

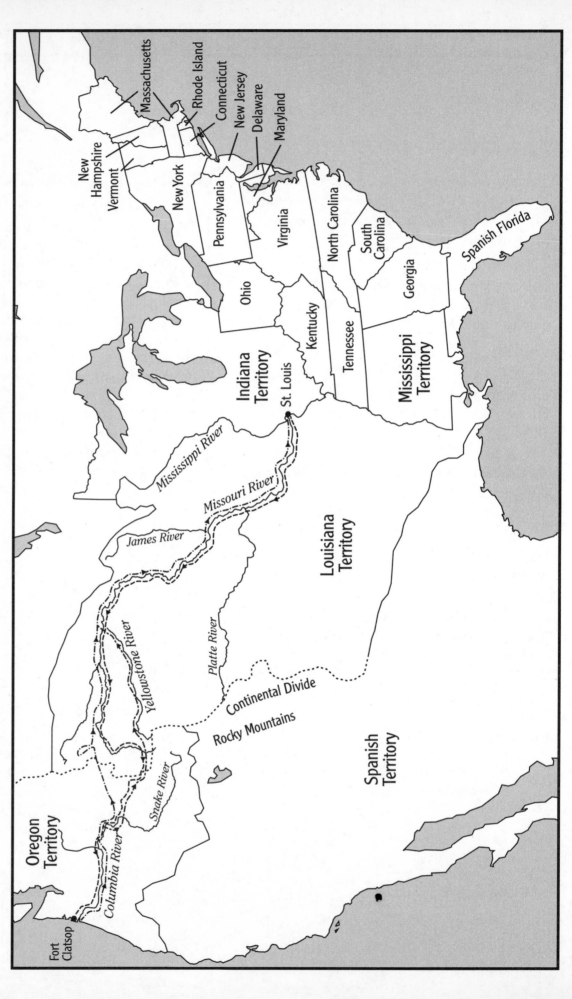

New Hampshire
Vermont
Massachusetts
Rhode Island
Connecticut
New Jersey
Delaware
Maryland
New York
Pennsylvania
Virginia
North Carolina
South Carolina
Georgia
Spanish Florida
Ohio
Kentucky
Tennessee
Mississippi Territory
Indiana Territory
St. Louis
Mississippi River
Missouri River
James River
Louisiana Territory
Platte River
Yellowstone River
Continental Divide
Rocky Mountains
Spanish Territory
Snake River
Oregon Territory
Columbia River
Fort Clatsop

The United States Today

Alaska

Hawaii

Washington
Oregon
California
Nevada
Idaho
Montana
North Dakota
Minnesota
Arizona
Utah
Wyoming
New Mexico
Colorado
Nebraska
South Dakota
Texas
Oklahoma
Kansas
Iowa
Wisconson
Michigan
Louisiana
Arkansas
Missouri
Illinois
Indiana
Michigan
Mississippi
Alabama
Tennessee
Kentucky
Ohio
West Virginia
Pennsylvania
New York
Vermont
New Hampshire
Maine
Georgia
South Carolina
North Carolina
Virginia
Florida
Washington, D.C.
Maryland
Delaware
New Jersey
Connecticut
Rhode Island
Massachusetts

Homemade Butter

Churning butter was a time-consuming task for pioneers. Creating their own butter will help students appreciate the effort once required to make something that today we can simply purchase at the store. The butter made here tastes great on johnny cakes (recipe found on page 28).

What to Do

1. Let the cream sit for a couple of hours until it is room temperature. Pour the cream into the jar and replace the lid tightly.

2. Get a good grip on the jar and shake it vigorously. You can demonstrate this for the class or have students each take a turn shaking the jar. After a few minutes, the sides will become coated with thick cream, and it will feel as if nothing is moving inside. But keep shaking. After a few more minutes, the cream will collect in lumps that you'll be able to see floating in liquid. The lumps are butter and the liquid is buttermilk.

3. Open the jar and drain off the liquid. You can save the buttermilk to drink if you wish, or discard it.

4. Put the butter in a colander and run it under cold water. Continue rinsing the butter until the water runs clear. Rinsing removes any remaining buttermilk, which, if left in the butter, will turn it sour.

5. Transfer the butter to a bowl and stir it with a spoon. Press the butter against the sides of the bowl to remove any remaining liquid and drain it off. Add the salt and stir well.

6. Smooth out the butter and use a toothpick to draw a design on top if you wish. Pioneers used to put their butter into wooden molds with pretty designs carved in them. When they removed the butter, the design was molded on top. Store your butter in a refrigerator until ready to use.

What You Need for About a Dozen Students:

- ◆ measuring spoons
- ◆ jar with lid (a spaghetti sauce jar works well)
- ◆ colander
- ◆ spoon
- ◆ empty butter bowl with lid, toothpick

Recipe Ingredients:

- ◆ ½ pint heavy cream
- ◆ ⅛ teaspoon salt

Better Butter

In *The Wagon Train* (Crabtree, 1999), author Bobbie Kalman says the pioneers found a better way to make butter. All they had to do was hang a bucket of cream from their wagons. The constant motion agitated the milk just as churning did. By the end of the day, the pioneers had butter—without all the hand churning!

The Civil War: America Divided

While pioneers were staking their claims in the West, the United States was beginning to split apart in the East. Lifestyles and politics in the agrarian South varied greatly from those in the more industrialized North. While Northern industry relied on cheap labor, Southern plantations were run using slave labor.

Slavery was at the heart of Southern dissension, but it was only one part of the overall issue of states' rights. Southerners believed that the federal government shouldn't have more power than the states. In addition, they were angered over government-imposed tariffs that made it more expensive to buy goods from Europe. These tariffs essentially forced Southern states to buy from the North. Southern separatists also argued that states had a right to secede, or leave, from the Union if they chose to. The 1860 election of

Abraham Lincoln, who championed keeping the Union intact, only worsened the rift. By Lincoln's inauguration in 1861, the states of South Carolina, Georgia, Alabama, Florida, Mississippi, Louisiana, and Texas had seceded from the Union. Soon, Virginia, North Carolina, Tennessee, and Arkansas joined the newly formed Confederate States of America.

When Confederates attacked federal troops at Fort Sumter in South Carolina, the Civil War began. Many thought the war would be short-lived. But it dragged on for four bloody years, claiming the lives of more than 600,000 Americans, more than in any other war in which the United States participated. Although they were outnumbered almost two to one, Southern armies led by General Robert E. Lee and other generals managed to defeat Union troops in many

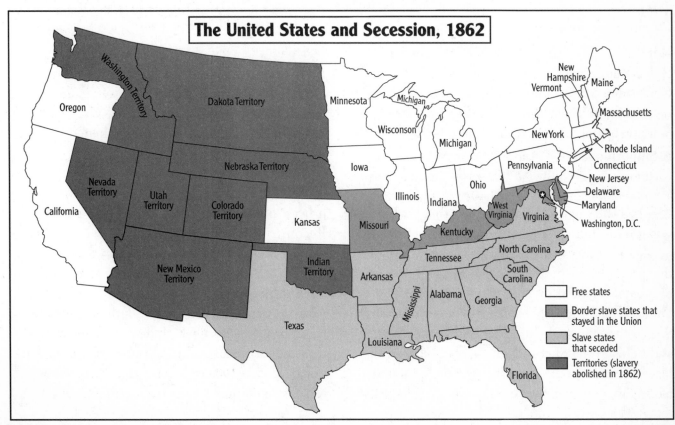

The United States and Secession, 1862

Washington Territory • Oregon • Dakota Territory • Minnesota • Michigan • New Hampshire • Vermont • Maine • Wisconsin • Michigan • Massachusetts • Nevada Territory • Nebraska Territory • Iowa • New York • Rhode Island • Utah Territory • Colorado Territory • Illinois • Indiana • Ohio • Pennsylvania • Connecticut • New Jersey • Delaware • California • Kansas • Missouri • West Virginia • Virginia • Maryland • Washington, D.C. • New Mexico Territory • Indian Territory • Kentucky • Tennessee • North Carolina • Arkansas • South Carolina • Mississippi • Alabama • Georgia • Texas • Louisiana • Florida

Free states
Border slave states that stayed in the Union
Slave states that seceded
Territories (slavery abolished in 1862)

Time Line

1820 Missouri Compromise ensures that the balance of slave states and free states is maintained

1857 Dred Scott decision, in which the Supreme Court rules that slaves are property and have no rights

1860 Abraham Lincoln elected president; South Carolina secedes from the Union

1861 Confederates fire on Fort Sumter

1863 Lincoln issues Emancipation Proclamation; Battle of Gettysburg fought; Lincoln delivers Gettysburg Address

1865 Confederate General Robert E. Lee surrenders to Union General Ulysses S. Grant at Appomattox Courthouse, Virginia; President Lincoln is assassinated; ratification of the Thirteenth Amendment frees the slaves

1868 Ratification of Fourteenth Amendment makes former slaves American citizens

1870 All Confederate states are readmitted to the Union

1877 Reconstruction ends

battles. In 1863, Lincoln issued the Emancipation Proclamation, which freed slaves living in the Confederacy. Six months later, the battle at Gettysburg, Pennsylvania, became a turning point, crushing Confederate hopes of driving the war into the Northern states.

In 1864, Lincoln appointed Ulysses S. Grant general in chief of the Union army. Grant changed the way the Civil War was fought. He was not hesitant to wage the kind of total war needed to destroy the South. Grant knew one of the strengths of the Union army was its superior numbers. Grant also sent generals William T. Sherman and Philip Sheridan to wage war against Southern civilians. While Sheridan burned homes and fields in the Shenandoah Valley, Sherman blazed a similar trail of destruction on his way to Savannah, Georgia, burning the city of Atlanta as

he went. The lack of food and resources combined with dwindling numbers of troops forced General Robert E. Lee to surrender to Grant at Appomattox Courthouse, Virginia, in 1865. President Lincoln was assassinated just five days later.

With the defeat of the Confederacy, slaves finally were freed in all states. In 1865, the process of rebuilding the South, known as Reconstruction, began. In order to reenter the Union, Southern states were required to ratify the Fourteenth Amendment, which made all former slaves American citizens. Resentment toward African Americans led many Southern states to pass Jim Crow laws, which discriminated against these new citizens and legalized segregation. Such practices later fueled the civil rights movement to win fair and equal treatment for all citizens.

Additional Resources

- *Addy's Cook Book* by Jodi Evert (Pleasant Company Publications, 1994)

- *Addy's Craft Book* by Rebecca Sample Bernstein and Jodi Evert (Pleasant Company Publications, 1994)

- *The American Civil War Homepage*
http://sunsite.utk.edu/civil-war/warweb.html
This site contains numerous resources, images, and links.

- *The Civil War: A Literature Approach* by Janet Cassidy (Scholastic, 1995) features literature-based activities for grades 4–8.

- *Cobblestone*, April 1981: "Highlights of the Civil War 1861–1865"

- *Cobblestone*, May 1887: "The Civil War: Reconstruction"

- *Food and Recipes of the Civil War* by George Erdosh (Powerkids Press, 1998)

- *Quilting Activities Across the Curriculum* by Wendy Buchberg (Scholastic, 1996)

- *The Underground Railroad*
www.nationalgeographic.org/features/99/railroad
This National Geographic Web site feature allows students to take a virtual trip north to freedom.

- *Valley of the Shadow: Two Communities in the American Civil War*
http://jefferson.village.Virginia.EDU/vshadow2
This site, which looks at the war from the views of two counties on opposite sides of the Mason-Dixon Line: Augusta County, Virginia, and Franklin County, Pennsylvania, contains original materials from the period and extensive activities.

An Eagle of War

One member of the Eighth Regiment of the Wisconsin Volunteer Infantry literally flew into battle. That's because he was a bald eagle named Old Abe. Old Abe became the mascot of the Eighth Regiment when he was just an eaglet, but he performed like a seasoned soldier in the thirty-some battles that he saw. The bird was a source of inspiration to the men of his regiment as he soared over their ranks in battle, calling out as if urging them on. Abe survived the war to become a living symbol of the Union, touring the country and delighting crowds wherever he went.

A Clan Formed in Hate

The Ku Klux Klan formed in Tennessee in 1866 for the purpose of fostering white supremacy and oppressing African Americans. Klansmen dressed in white robes and hoods and terrorized African Americans by burning their homes and promoting violence, including whippings and murder. In only a year, the Klan and its mission of hate had spread to all the Southern states.

Toy That Tricks the Eye

Students may believe that animation began with
Walt Disney, but its roots actually go back
to the 1800s. Paul Roget invented the
thaumatrope in 1828. It was an optical
toy that worked because of what is called
persistence of vision: The brain remembers what the eyes see for a split second
after the image is gone. Because of this,
animated pictures, which are a series of still
images shown in very quick succession, appear to move
seamlessly. The concept can be demonstrated by making
and playing with a thaumatrope, a toy that had become
popular by Civil War times.

What to Do

Once students have made their own thaumatropes, and
had a chance to use them, ask students to think about
how they really work. Explain that even though the bee
and hive are really separate, they appear to be in one
picture because of persistence of vision.

What You Need For Each Student:
- copy of the pattern and directions, page 45
- markers
- glue
- thin cardboard
- scissors
- hole punch
- 2 rubber bands

Toy That Tricks the Eye

What You Need:
- pattern, below
- markers
- glue
- thin cardboard
- scissors
- hole punch
- 2 rubber bands

Directions

1. Color the bee and hive designs on the thaumatrope circles and cut them out.

2. Glue the hive circle to a thin piece of cardboard. Trim the cardboard to match the circle. Apply glue to the back of the bee circle and attach it to the other side of the cardboard, matching dot with dot and square with square.

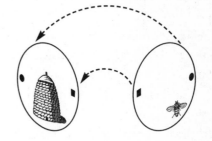

3. Punch holes through the cardboard at the dots and squares. Then loop a rubber band through each hole as shown.

4. Hold the thaumatrope with the hive facing you. Holding each rubber band, turn the thaumatrope in one direction to wind it up tightly. Keep it at arm's length and let go to see the bee and hive appear as one picture.

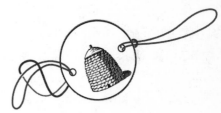

5. Why do you think the bee and hive appear to be in one picture even though they are really separate?

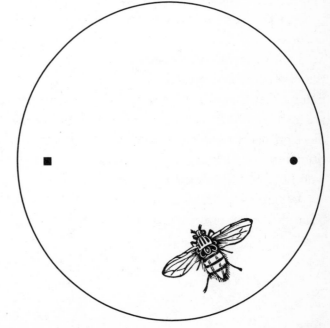

Boats Across Battle Lines

After the battle of Fredericksburg, Virginia, in 1862, Union troops occupied one side of the Rappahannock River while Confederate forces occupied the city on the other side. Even though it was illegal, soldiers on both sides sent makeshift miniature boats across the river to barter for such goods as tobacco, coffee, sugar, and postage stamps. A boat carrying tobacco from the Confederate shore might be named after a Southern ironclad. When the boat returned bearing coffee or some other Union commodity, it might be renamed after one of the Union's ships!

This amiable exchange says a lot about the Civil War. Men who were neighbors, even brothers, were suddenly at odds with each other. Even though politics and ideology caused the two sides to clash, something as simple as the desire for a good cup of coffee could still bring men together. Making miniature boats and writing messages to the "other side" can give students a feel for one of the dichotomies that existed during the Civil War.

What to Do

Explain how soldiers sent messages and traded goods across enemy lines in Fredericksburg during the Civil War. Share accounts of this story with the class from *Rebels Resurgent: Fredericksburg to Chancellorsville* (Time-Life, 1987). Ask students why they think soldiers were willing to talk to and trade with the enemy. Do students think it would have been difficult for soldiers to fight later against the same men with whom they had been friends?

Help students make boats out of empty milk cartons, using the reproducible instructions on page 47. Boats can be made from many other throwaway items. Small blocks of wood, for example, are also good boat bases and enhance the idea that Civil War soldiers probably used wood to make their boats at Fredericksburg. Students can stick one end of a straw in modeling clay on the wood block, then attach a paper sail.

When it's time to sail the boats, if there is not a convenient pond, fountain, or creek, try using a small wading pool.

What You Need for Each Student:
- copy of the directions, page 47
- empty milk carton or block of wood
- plastic straw
- paper
- scissors
- tape
- modeling clay
- glue
- marker
- paints and brushes
  OPTIONAL

Boats Across Battle Lines

What You Need:
♦ empty milk carton
♦ plastic straw
♦ paper
♦ scissors
♦ tape
♦ glue
♦ marker

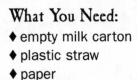

Directions

1. Cut one side out of an empty milk carton, as shown.

2. Tape a plastic straw to the front of the boat and use the cut-out section of the carton as a sail.

3. Cut two slits in the sail as shown, and poke the straw through.

4. Write a message to someone on the "other side" and put it in the boat.

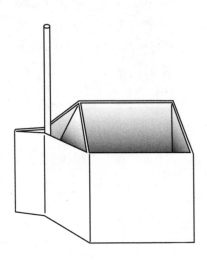

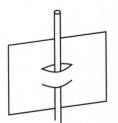

5. Don't forget to christen the boats! The initials *U.S.S.*, which stands for *United States Ship*, preceded the names of federal naval vessels, while Confederate vessels were preceded by *C.S.S.* for *Confederate States Ship*.

6. Float the boats in a pond, fountain, or nearby creek.

7. Learn about some real Civil War ships. Ironclads such as the *Monitor* and *Virginia* featured cutting-edge technology at the time. Steamers were also fairly new additions. There was even a submarine. The *Hunley* was a Confederate sub propelled by manpower—several men cranked it from inside the ship.

Underground Railroad Quilt Patch

During the Civil War, some quilts were much more than warm blankets—they served as "signposts" on the Underground Railroad. The Underground Railroad was neither a railroad nor underground. It was a system of getting slaves north to freedom. Harriet Tubman was the most famous "conductor" on the Underground Railroad, helping more than 300 slaves reach their destination.

Slaves traveled many routes out of the South to freedom in the North or Canada. Along the way were stopovers at the homes and businesses of abolitionists who would help "passengers" proceed to their next stop. Even after reaching the Northern states, passengers weren't always safe. Laws were passed that required escaped slaves to be returned to their owners. So passengers often traveled at night and had to rely on signs and symbols to know where and how to proceed.

Underground Railroad passengers looked to the stars to guide them north. Signs such as lit lanterns or tools left in a certain way let travelers know whether to keep going or where to stop. Quilts were one of the more creative signposts. A quilt with a specific pattern might be aired outside as a message for slaves to get ready for their journey. Other patterns let slaves know that they'd reached a safe house. One children's story, *Sweet Clara and the Freedom Quilt*, tells of a slave girl who made a quilt that was really a map designed to lead slaves to the Underground Railroad.

By making quilt pieces students will see how these "signposts" helped slaves reach freedom.

What You Need for Each Student or Pair:

- ♦ copy of the map and directions, page 49
- ♦ construction paper or fabric scraps
- ♦ scissors
- ♦ glue
- ♦ bulletin board paper
- ♦ maps or atlas
- ♦ reference books
- ♦ highlighters or colored pencils

What to Do

Discuss the Underground Railroad and how quilts were used as signals to the "passengers." Visit the Web site of the National Geographic Society at **www.nationalgeographic.org/features/99/railroad** for a virtual trip along the Railroad. Show students pictures of quilts with a variety of different patterns. A good source for illustrated quilt patterns is *Encyclopedia of Pieced Quilt Patterns* by Barbara Brackman (Collector Books, 1993).

Examine the Underground Railroad routes shown on reproducible page 49. As a class, select a route using maps to identify each section along the way. Have the class design a quilt "map" to lead runaway slaves to safety. Divide the route into sections (at least nine). Assign each section to one or two students. You can assign more sections, but be sure the number you make will form a complete "quilt" when assembled.

Henry "Box" Brown

One slave came up with an ingenious, if not risky, way to reach the North. Henry Brown had himself boxed inside a crate and shipped to Philadelphia. Despite a bumpy ride, he got out safe and free—but with a new nickname!

Underground Railroad Quilt Patch

Directions

1. On the map below, highlight the Underground Railroad route for which your class has chosen to make a quilt to help runaway slaves reach safety. Draw a star next to the section of the route that your patch represents.

2. Use maps to look up places along your section of the route and choose landmarks that would help travelers know when they've reached their destination. Or come up with a design that indicates direction. Use traditional quilt patterns or create new ones. Don't be too obvious in your design. You don't want to give away any Underground Railroad passengers!

3. Make the designs using construction paper or fabric scraps glued onto an 8½-inch by 8½-inch square. Arrange the squares to "read" from left to right and top to bottom, just like words on a page. Glue the finished pieces to a backing of bulletin-board paper.

4. Hang up the finished quilt proudly as a "signpost" from your class.

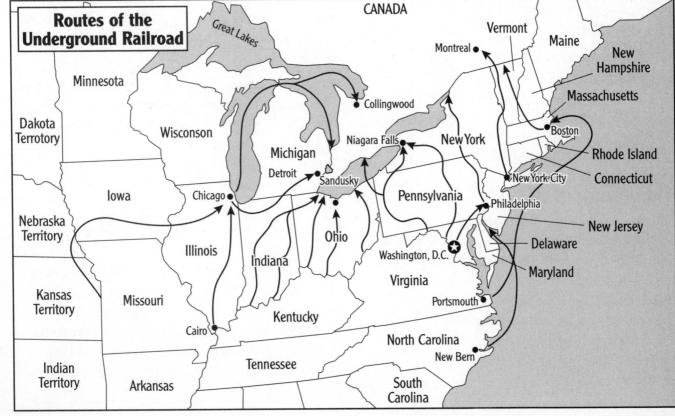

Parlor Games

Without television or video games, what did people do for entertainment in the late nineteenth century? Sometimes they played parlor games: simple games that required no special equipment, only several willing participants. They are called parlor games because they were often played in the parlor, where people entertained guests. Here are some parlor games that were enjoyed during happier times of the Civil War era.

Cupid's Coming

All players choose a letter of the alphabet to start the game. The first player says, "Cupid's coming." The second player asks, "How is he coming?" To which the first player must answer with a word beginning with the chosen letter and ending in *ing*. For example, if the chosen letter is *f*, the player might answer, "Flying!" Play continues with the second player saying, "Cupid's coming." To which the third player asks, "How?" Players must answer using a word beginning with the chosen letter until someone can no longer think of a word. Then players choose a new letter and begin again.

Yes and No

One player thinks of a person, place, or thing, and the rest of the group take turns asking questions, trying to discover who, where, or what it is. To each question, the player answers only yes or no. Questions should be framed to help narrow down the possibilities.

Blindman's Buff

One person is It and is blindfolded with a handkerchief or scarf and positioned in the center of the rest of the group. The others spin It around three times, then scamper off. The blindfolded player must then attempt to find and tag one of the others, who then becomes It for the next game. Take care when playing this game so that the blindfolded player doesn't bump into anything.

Guess My Number

The American Boy's Book of Sports and Games first printed in 1864 describes three ways to astonish guests by determining a randomly picked number. In the process, students can sharpen their math skills. Depending on their skill level, you can direct them to think of one-, two-, or three-digit numbers.

Game 1 A person thinks of a number (example: 8). The guesser then asks the person to do the following: Multiply the number by 3 (*24*); add 1 (*25*); multiply by 3 (*75*); add that amount to the original number (*83*) and announce the total. The guesser knows that this combination of equations always results in a number ending in 3. By simply eliminating the 3 from the ones place, the original number remains (*8*).

Game 2 A person thinks of a number (example: 8). The guesser then asks the person to do the following: Double the number (*16*); add 4 (*20*); multiply by 5 (*100*); add 12 (*112*); multiply by 10 (*1120*) and reveal the total. The guesser subtracts 320 (*800*) and strikes off the two 0s to reveal the original number (*8*).

Game 3 A person thinks of a number (example: 8). The guesser then asks the person to do the following: Multiply the number by itself (*64*); subtract 1 from the original number thought of (*7*); multiply that number by itself (*49*); subtract the second result from the first (*64 – 49 = 15*) and reveal the total. The guesser then adds 1 to the total (*16*) and divides that sum by 2 to determine the original number (*8*).

Wartime Tunes

You may already know that the "Battle Hymn of the Republic" was the anthem of the Union army, while Confederates marched to "Dixie." But there are many more wartime tunes that helped soldiers on both sides pass the time and reminisce about home. Studying the lyrics and hearing the music lets students listen to a piece of the past. Thanks to computer technology, children can visit Web sites and find both lyrics and audio files for several Civil War era songs. Two such sites are Music of the Civil War at **http://civilwarmidi.homepage.com** and Poetry and Music of the War Between the States at **http://users.erols.com/kfraser**. There you'll find songs from both the North and South, as well as popular music of the period. The Music of the Civil War site also features songs sung by slaves.

Note that the lyrics to war tunes sometimes contain mild profanity and references that may not be considered politically correct today. Keep in mind that these songs were sung by nineteenth-century soldiers! Before allowing students free access to any untoward lyrics, preview the sites and choose songs appropriate for your group. Then direct students to those songs in particular.

What to Do

1. Go to one of the Civil War music Web pages to sample audio files and print lyrics for songs from the Union and the Confederacy as well as slave songs and other music of the period. Links to other sites can be explored to learn more about the role of music in the war.

What You Need for Each Group of Students:
- ◆ computer with Internet access
- ◆ paper
- ◆ pens

2. Listen to the music and ask students to follow along with the lyrics. They should examine the lyrics closely to answer these questions:

- ◆ What are some differences between songs of the Union and songs of the Confederacy? In what ways are they similar? Give examples of both.

- ◆ Which songs "complain" about wartime life? Why would soldiers want to complain in songs?

- ◆ How do slave songs differ from the other melodies of the time in terms of both lyrics and music? Why do you think they are different?

- ◆ The purpose of some tunes was to keep soldiers marching or to encourage them in battle. In what ways are these tunes different from others of the period and why?

3. Break the class into groups of four or five students and assign each group a song to learn. Have a mini concert, then discuss the answers to the questions with the class.

4. As an extension to this activity, compare and contrast the Civil War songs with some from World War I or World War II.

Hardtack

Troops on both sides of the Civil War were issued hardtack, a bland type of cracker that was meant to travel well as field rations. Whereas Union soldiers were well supplied and had lots of food to eat besides hardtack, Confederate soldiers often had little else. After sampling hardtack, students will better understand why soldiers who had nothing else to eat really did have it hard.

What to Do

1. Preheat oven to 375°. Combine the salt and water in the mixing bowl and add the flour slowly, stirring well. Add flour until the dough is no longer sticky and can be handled.

2. Transfer dough to a floured surface and knead a minute or two, then roll out to about ½-inch thickness. Using a pizza cutter, cut dough into 3-inch by 3-inch pieces and transfer to a baking sheet. Use a fork to poke about 16 holes in each cracker.

3. Bake for about 60 minutes. Remove from the oven and cool completely before eating.

What You Need to Make One Batch of Hardtack (about 10 pieces):
- measuring cups and spoons
- large mixing bowl
- spoon
- rolling pin
- fork
- pizza cutter
- baking sheet

Recipe Ingredients:
- 1 tablespoon salt
- 1 cup water
- 6 cups flour (approximately)

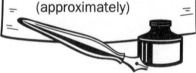

War Is No Picnic

At the first Battle of Manassas, Virginia, local folks were so confident of the Union's swift defeat of the Confederates that many of them dressed up and went out for picnics near the battlefield. When the Confederates advanced toward the picnic area, the spectators had to run for safety. The Confederate victory at Manassas proved that the war was not bound to be short-lived.

The Immigrant Experience and Industrial Revolution

After the Civil War, a great industrial revolution took place, bolstering the American economy, shifting much of the population from rural areas to cities, and opening the country to millions of immigrants. This revolution grew out of the mechanization of factories that had taken place in the North prior to the war. Some of the large industries that thrived at this time produced steel, oil, aluminum, and built the railroads that carried goods and people across the country.

This exponential growth in industry made many business owners fabulously wealthy. Some of these so-called robber barons sought to cement their companies' security by buying out competitors and establishing monopolies or trusts. At the same time, workers in many factories were toiling in unsafe and undesirable conditions. Young children could be used as laborers, and employees faced long workdays with low wages and few benefits such as sick leave or vacation. To protest unfair working practices, unions began to form. Organized workers were able to put pressure on company owners by threatening to strike. Eventually the influence of unions led to many reforms for laborers. The passage of the Sherman Anti-Trust Act in 1890 helped end the reign of monopolies and trusts.

The booming American economy drew immigrants in record numbers—21 million came between 1870 and 1910. It was the largest movement of people in history. Most of the immigrants came from Europe. New York alone was the port of entry for more than 16 million men, women, and children. Passage of a law limiting immigration in 1924 effectively ended the great migration.

In 1898, the U.S. battleship *Maine* was struck and destroyed off the coast of Cuba during that island's rebellion against Spain. What actually happened to the ship is unknown, but the incident fueled a desire among Americans to enter the conflict and help liberate the people of Cuba. The Spanish-American War was fought both in the Philippines, which was a Spanish colony, and in Puerto Rico. Defeat of Spanish troops in both places ended the war quickly. As a result, the United States acquired Puerto Rico, Guam, and the Philippines, while Cuba gained its independence from Spain. And Theodore Roosevelt became a national hero when he led his cavalry of Rough Riders to victory at San Juan Hill.

Time Line

1867 United States buys Alaska from Russia

1869 Transcontinental Railroad completed

1876 Alexander Graham Bell invents the telephone

1879 Thomas Edison invents the lightbulb

1886 American Federation of Labor (AFL) formed

1890 Sherman Anti-Trust Act passed

1898 Spanish-American War

1901 Theodore Roosevelt becomes president upon the assassination of William McKinley

Additional Resources

♦ *Cobblestone*, September 1981: "America at Work: The Industrial Revolution"

♦ *Cobblestone*, December 1982: "American Immigrants: Part 1"

♦ *Cobblestone*, January 1983: "American Immigrants: Part 2"

♦ *Ellis Island*
www.ellisisland.org
This site offers information and images about this port of entry for millions of immigrants.

♦ *Ellis Island* by Catherine Reef (Dillon Press, 1991)

♦ *HistoryChannel.com*
www.historychannel.com/ellisisland
This Web site offers a virtual tour of the immigrant experience at Ellis Island.

♦ *Immigration Then and Now* by Karen Baiker (Scholastic, 1997) is an activity guide, audiocassette, and poster for grades 4–8.

♦ *Inventors and Inventions* by Lorraine Hopping Egan (Scholastic, 1997) is an activity guide and poster for grades 4–8.

♦ *National Inventors Hall of Fame*
www.invent.org
This site has biographies of numerous inventors, images of exhibits, audio clips, and links.

♦ *Kids' Inventor Resources*
www.InventorEd.org/k-12
This Web page links students to sites and resources devoted to invention.

♦ *Samantha's Cook Book* (Pleasant Company Publications, 1998)

♦ *Samantha's Craft Book* (Pleasant Company Publications, 1994)

The Real McCoy

Elijah McCoy was born to escaped slaves who had traveled on the Underground Railroad from Kentucky to Canada. After moving back to the United States, his parents saved enough money to send Elijah to Scotland to study engineering. When he returned home a fully qualified engineer, the only job Elijah could get was as a fireman (the man who fueled train furnaces) with the Michigan Central Railroad. But he soon became famous for his 1872 invention that allowed trains' moving parts to be oiled without stopping the engine. Oiling steam engines had been dangerous for workers and wasted lots of time. His invention was so popular that customers insisted on the "real McCoy." He ultimately founded the Elijah McCoy Manufacturing Company and earned more than 50 patents.

Inspiration and Perspiration

Thomas Edison once said that "genius is one percent inspiration and 99 percent perspiration." The activity that follows will allow students to sweat out some creative ideas, using small items that can be "recycled" into something else. In the process they are bound to come away with an appreciation for inventors like Edison and Alexander Graham Bell, whose genius flowered during our country's age of industry.

What to Do

1. Divide the class into groups of four or five and give an inspiration box to each group. Explain that students are a "think tank" of inventors who must come up with at least one invention made from the items in the box. Remind students that each group is not just working for itself but is part of a class contest to create the best invention using as many parts from the box as possible.

2. Allow the groups a fixed amount of time to work on their creations, then stop everyone. Each group should present its invention to the class and explain how it works. After the presentations, give students the opportunity to vote on their favorite invention. You can award a small prize to the winning group if you like. You also may want to reward the group that used the most parts from its inspiration box.

3. Children can expand their knowledge of inventions by researching an item invented during the age of industry and presenting a brief report to the class. The National Inventors Hall of Fame Web site at **www.invent.org** is a great place to start.

Suggested Items for an Inspiration Box for Each Group of Students:
- shoe box or other lidded container
- string
- rubber bands
- tape
- glue
- paper
- cardboard
- spools
- wire
- plastic cups
- bottle caps
- paper clips

Each box should contain the same number of each item.

Age of Inventors

The late 1800s saw the invention of the telephone by Alexander Graham Bell and the successful construction of the car by Henry Ford. But it was Thomas Alva Edison who was unsurpassed for sheer inventiveness. In addition to creating the electric lightbulb, he patented the phonograph, a movie camera, an electric railroad, a generator, and nearly 2,000 other inventions. It seems appropriate that one of Edison's inventions—the lightbulb—became the symbol for having a bright idea.

Leaf-Print Cards

Scientific study blossomed at the same time that the world was becoming industrialized. Charles Darwin wrote about his theory of evolution in 1859, while the discovery and study of fossils of dinosaurs and other ancient creatures led scientists to question not only how old life on Earth might be but also how it developed over the ages. The average person living in the late nineteenth century might not be able to study fossils, but he or she could view the plants and animals that lived nearby. It was common to sketch nature's beauty as part of such study. John James Audubon's paintings of the birds he observed are but one example of how art and science merged.

The cards that follow, made from impressions of leaves, are not only beautiful to look at but also a lesson in botany.

What to Do

Take students outside to collect leaves from various trees, shrubs, or other plants. Don't collect leaves from private property without permission, or from any plants that might be rare or poisonous.

What You Need for Each Student:

- ◆ copy of directions, page 57
- ◆ light-colored 8½-inch by 11-inch paper
- ◆ ruler
- ◆ scissors
- ◆ fresh leaves of various types
- ◆ newspaper
- ◆ heavy book
- ◆ paint
- ◆ brushes
- ◆ water

Leaf-Print Cards

Fun and Easy American History Crafts and Games   Scholastic Professional Books

Directions

1. Collect a few leaves.

2. If the leaves are curly, cover them with newspaper and place a heavy book on top for a few minutes.

3. Cut cards out of light-colored paper. Use a ruler to draw a line dividing an 8½-inch by 11-inch sheet of paper into two 8½-inch by 5½-inch pieces. Cut the pieces apart and then fold each in half to form a 4¼-inch by 5½-inch card.

4. Place a flattened leaf on newspaper and brush paint on the surface that is the most "bumpy." Don't use too much paint or it will run.

5. Make a test printing on a piece of newspaper by placing the leaf paint-side down onto the paper. Once you achieve the desired results on the newspaper, use the leaves to make images on the outsides of the cards.

6. Press the leaf gently to make sure it makes full contact with the card, being careful not to let the leaf slide or shift, which will blur the image. You may need to adjust the amount of paint applied if the image is too faint or too blotched. Try using two or more colors and several different types of leaves. Allow the paint to dry completely before writing inside the cards.

What You Need:
- light-colored 8½-inch by 11-inch paper
- ruler
- scissors
- fresh leaves of various types
- newspaper
- heavy book
- paint
- brushes
- water

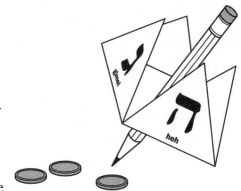

Dreidel

Between 1880 and 1910, more than two million Jews immigrated to the United States. Like other immigrants during the great migration, they sought to create a better life for themselves in their new home. In Eastern Europe, Jews faced many hardships because of their religion. America gave them a chance to flee persecution and to practice their religious beliefs freely.

Jews brought with them their special holidays, celebrations, and customs. One custom, the dreidel game, is played during Hanukkah, the Jewish Festival of Lights. Hanukkah celebrates the defeat of King Antiochus IV Epiphanes of Syria, and the rededication of the Jewish temple after that victory.

What to Do

Explain that the names of the four letters are *nun, gimel, heh* (hay), and *shin*. They stand for the words *Nes gadol hayah sham,* which mean "A great miracle happened there." The miracle took place after the victory of Judas Maccabeus over Antiochus, when the temple's holy oil, which should have lasted only one day, burned instead for eight.

What You Need for Each Student:
♦ copy of the pattern and directions, page 59
♦ scissors
♦ sharpened pencil
♦ dried beans or pennies to use as *gelt* (the Yiddish word for "money")

Steerage Sums

Even though steerage passengers may have paid only $30 each for a ticket, the ships that carried them made a lot of money because they could pack so many people in a single vessel—up to 2,000 in some cases. Here is a calculation for your students to try. If a ship could carry 2,000 steerage passengers at $30 each, how much money would it collect in one trip? ($60,000)

Dreidel

What You Need:
♦ scissors
♦ sharpened pencil
♦ dried beans or pennies to use as *gelt* (the Yiddish word for "money")

Directions

1. Cut out the dreidel pattern around the solid lines. Fold the dreidel along the dotted lines, as shown, so that the Hebrew letters face outward.

2. Poke the sharp end of a pencil through the center of the square section of the dreidel. The sides with the Hebrew letters should point up toward the pencil's eraser, and the pencil tip should stick out beneath the dreidel.

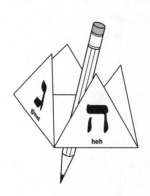

3. To play the game, get into groups of four or five. Each player puts two pieces of *gelt* into the pot to start. Then players take turns spinning the dreidel and adding or removing gelt as dictated by the spins. The character that lands facing up after the spin determines what happens.

   nun: Nothing happens and the next player takes a turn.

   gimel: The player takes the whole pot, and the game starts over, if desired.

   heh: The player takes half the pot.

   shin: The player puts one piece of gelt in the pot.

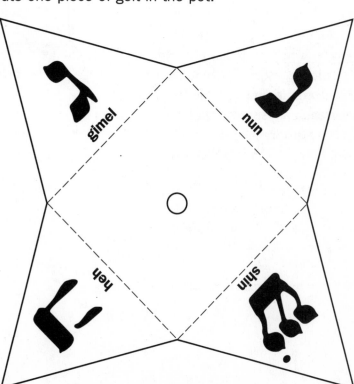

Tangram

Not all immigrants came to the United States through New York. Thousands of Chinese immigrants came across the Pacific Ocean to California. Like many others, they were lured to America by the prospect of gold. After the Gold Rush subsided, many Chinese workers went on to help build the Transcontinental Railroad. Life was not easy for Chinese Americans. They were originally denied citizenship and the protection of laws that benefited others. In 1882, Congress passed the Chinese Exclusion Act, which banned immigration of Chinese laborers to the United States until the act was repealed in 1943. Still the Chinese who came to America helped make our nation what it is today.

The game of tangram that follows is but one small contribution of Chinese culture to American society.

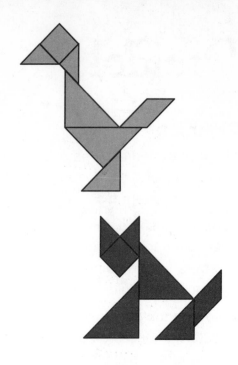

What to Do

1. Pass out a copy of the tangram puzzle on page 61 to each student and let the kids color the shapes, glue them onto cardboard, and cut them out.

2. Explain that tangram is a puzzle in which you must use all seven shapes to make a design. All of the shapes must touch, but none should overlap.

3. If you like, you can hold a tangram match. The object is to see who can make a given shape fastest. Kids can play individually or in teams. Toss out a challenge—such as making a bird, flower, or toy—and see who comes up with a design using all seven shapes fastest. A variation to "speed" tangrams is to allot a certain time limit to the creative process—say, three minutes—and let kids judge the best designs after time's up.

What You Need for Each Student:

♦ copy of pattern and directions, page 61
♦ markers
♦ thin cardboard
♦ glue
♦ scissors

Tangram

Directions

What You Need:
♦ markers
♦ thin cardboard
♦ glue
♦ scissors

1. Use markers to color the tangram shapes, if desired. Glue the square to a piece of thin cardboard. Then cut out the shapes.

2. The object of tangram is to make as many different shapes from the seven pieces, or tans, as possible. Experiment with the shapes. Can you create an animal? A person's face? A building?

3. After playing with the tans, see if you can put them back together to form a square.

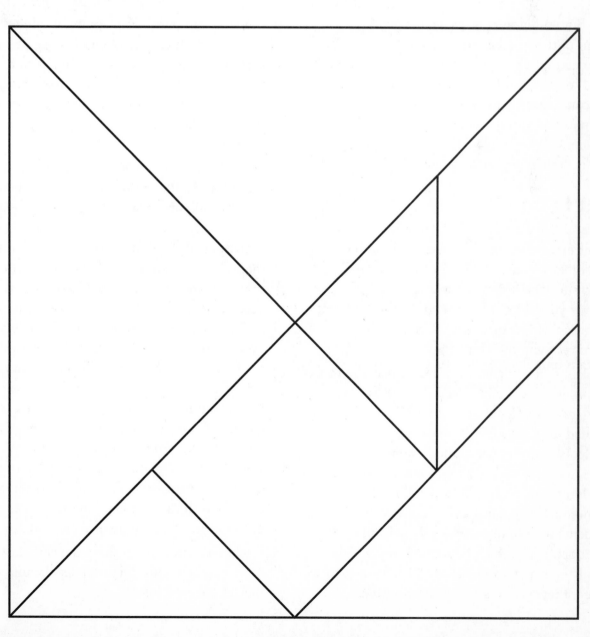

Pack Your Bag

The promise of freedom and opportunity brought millions of immigrants to the United States between 1860 and 1920. Most of them had little money and made their way from Europe by traveling in steerage, often on ships that might hold as many as 2,000 such passengers. The conditions were crowded, dirty, and uncomfortable for a journey that could last from just over a week to as long as two months, depending on the type of ship. Many fell ill and some passengers died en route. But immigrants were encouraged by thought of the new lives they would soon begin.

No matter where they came from, immigrants needed to leave most of their past lives behind. They could bring only what necessities they could carry, plus one family item of value—a musical instrument, for example. How would your students prepare for such a journey?

What to Do

1. Give students a chance to learn what the immigrant experience was like by examining books and other resources. The History Channel Web site, **www.historychannel.com/ellisisland**, features a virtual journey through Ellis Island that paints a vivid picture of what immigrants faced upon reaching the United States.

2. Explain that students are going to play the role of immigrants coming to the United States in the late 1800s. Their job? To pack the items needed for their life in a new country. Remind students that they are limited to one or two bags, which would be all they could carry on the long journey. In addition, each family is allowed to bring one item of value. Give students time to discuss with their families what necessities they should pack and which family heirloom or object they would want to take if they were making such a journey.

What You Need for Each Student:
- research materials
- Internet access OPTIONAL
- file folder
- construction or scrap paper
- tape
- staple
- scissors
- pens

3. Students can put their planning to the test. At home, have them actually pack a bag or two with the items they want to bring. Can they fit them all in? Remind them that everything must go in one or two bags that they can carry on their own. Discuss the children's experiences the next day.

4. Students can then make a "suitcase" by taping the sides of a file folder together and cutting paper handles to staple to the open edge of the folder. Next, students can cut out paper representations of the things they will bring with them. For example, a small cut-out shirt can represent the shirts they will bring. On the paper cutout, write the number of shirts packed and put it in the suitcase. Remind students that they are packing for a sea trip that takes several weeks. And the things they bring will have to serve them in their new home. There will be little room for anything that isn't necessary. Continue cutting out items and filling the suitcase until everything is included. Finally, students should make a representation of the one family item that they will take to the new country with them. They can bring in a photo of this object from home if they want.

5. Encourage students to share the contents of their suitcases with the group, explaining why they chose each item.

German-Style Cookies

German immigrants brought Christmas traditions that shaped the way many Americans have celebrated the holiday ever since. The decorated Christmas tree (tannenbaum) is the most notable addition, but other German influences include advent calendars and special Christmas breads and cookies. The recipe that follows makes festive cookies in the German tradition. Your students can make the dough in class and, if needed, take some home to bake.

What to Do

1. Preheat oven to 375°. Spray baking sheets with nonstick cooking spray.

2. Cream the butter, sugar, egg, egg yolk, and lemon juice until fluffy.

3. Combine the flour, baking powder, salt, cinnamon, nutmeg, and cloves. Pour this mixture into the creamed batter and stir until well mixed and smooth. Dough should be firm and easy to handle. If dough is too sticky to handle, add a small amount of flour.

4. Lightly flour a flat surface and roll out the dough to 1/16-inch thickness. Cut with a star-shaped cookie cutter. Place cookies on the baking sheets. Beat the egg white until it's bubbly and brush the tops of the cookies with it.

5. Bake at 375° for 6 to 8 minutes.

Imported Holidays

German Christmas festivities aren't the only holiday traditions that made their way into American culture. Halloween customs of dressing in costume, trick-or-treating, and carving jack-o'-lanterns come from Ireland and date back to Gaelic roots some 3,000 years ago. Ancient people used to dress in costumes and offer goodies to appease the spirits of the dead, which they believed walked Earth on Halloween, or Samhain as it was called then. Jack-o'-lanterns come from the story of a man named Jack who was denied admittance to heaven or hell. Instead he was forced to walk Earth with only an ember from hell stuck in a turnip to light his way. Carved turnips soon gave way to pumpkins when the tradition came to the United States with Irish immigrants.

What You Need to Make 3½ Dozen Cookies:

- ♦ 2 mixing bowls
- ♦ measuring cups and spoons
- ♦ spoon
- ♦ baking sheets
- ♦ nonstick cooking spray
- ♦ rolling pin
- ♦ star-shaped cookie cutter
- ♦ spatula
- ♦ pastry brush

Recipe Ingredients:

- ♦ 1½ tablespoons butter or margarine
- ♦ ¾ cup white sugar
- ♦ 1 egg
- ♦ 1 egg yolk, reserve white
- ♦ ½ teaspoon lemon juice
- ♦ 1⅙ cups all-purpose flour
- ♦ 1¼ teaspoons baking powder
- ♦ ⅛ teaspoon salt
- ♦ ½ teaspoon ground cinnamon
- ♦ ⅛ teaspoon ground nutmeg
- ♦ ⅛ teaspoon ground cloves

The United States: Becoming a World Power

As the Industrial Revolution propelled the United States into the twentieth century, immigrants poured into the country at the greatest rate ever. But this growth and prosperity would soon be overshadowed by the specter of war. When the Austrian Archduke Franz Ferdinand was assassinated in Sarajevo, Serbia, Austria-Hungary attacked Serbia. Austria-Hungary was backed by its allies Germany and Italy, which were known as the Central Powers. Serbia was backed by Russia, and Russia by France. Britain and Belgium entered the conflict on the side of the French. The United States at first remained neutral. But when German U-boats sank the British ocean liner *Lusitania* and several unarmed American ships, President Woodrow Wilson prevailed on Congress to enter World War I in 1917 and fight for the Allies. When the war ended in 1918, the victorious Allies levied severe punishments on Germany, exacting money and territory and limiting the size of its army. Historians believe that these severe punishments embarrassed the Germans and ruined the country's economy, which probably led to the eventual rise of Adolf Hitler. After the war, the map of Europe was redrawn and several new countries were formed.

Back in the United States, women were fighting another type of battle—for the right to vote. The fight for women's suffrage had begun in the mid-1800s. But it wasn't until 1920 and the ratification of the Nineteenth Amendment that women were allowed to vote in national elections. Susan B. Anthony and Elizabeth Cady Stanton were key figures in the suffrage movement.

The 1920s were a decade of high times, marked by prosperity, artistic creativity, and a zest for life. But in 1929, the stock market crashed, taking with it the Roaring Twenties and ushering in the Great Depression. The market crashed because many people had invested their money unwisely, banks had offered credit too freely, and businesses had overproduced and flooded the market. Many who had invested their money in the stock market lost everything. More than 5,000 banks failed when people couldn't pay their loans, and one in three workers became jobless. When Franklin D. Roosevelt was elected president in 1932, the nation was still in the grips of the Depression. His New Deal used taxpayer money to fund programs designed to improve the economy. One of the programs was the Civilian Conservation Corps, which employed 25 million in environmental improvement projects. The Social Security Act of 1935 guaranteed benefits to orphans, the elderly, and those injured on the job.

Even with the New Deal, the economy did not recover until the United States entered World War II, and the demand for military equipment created new jobs and refueled the battered economy. World War II broke out after Germany, under the leadership of Adolf Hitler began

Flight Firsts

In 1903 two brothers who were bicycle mechanics made history when their airplane made the first sustained flight at Kitty Hawk, North Carolina. The Wright brothers' plane covered only 120 feet and stayed aloft for a brief 12 seconds on that first flight, but it launched the age of aviation. Only 11 years later, airplanes were already an important war machine as pilots engaged in "dogfights" over Europe.

conquering neighboring countries. Seeking to expand their territories, dictators in Italy and Japan also took control of their people with military force. At the same time, Germany waged a secret war against European Jews called the Holocaust. The Nazis rounded up Jews, Poles, and Gypsies and sent them to concentration camps where they were forced to work or were killed. More than six million Jews died in the Holocaust.

The Allies (Britain, China, and France) were united against the Axis powers (Germany, Italy, and Japan). The United States remained out of the conflict until Japan bombed Pearl Harbor, Hawaii, in 1941, and joined the Allies that year. Russia, which had sided with the Axis powers, joined the Allies in 1941 after Germany invaded the Soviet Union. The war continued for four years. On May 7, 1945, Germany surrendered.

And after the United States dropped the first atomic bombs on Hiroshima and Nagasaki in Japan, the war ended. To preserve peace worldwide, the United Nations was formed in 1945.

Additional Resources

- *Cobblestone*, March 1985: "Susan B. Anthony and the Beginning of the Women's Movement"
- *Cobblestone*, December 1985: "World War II: The Home Front"
- *Cobblestone*, June 1986: "World War I"
- *Events That Shaped the Century* (Time-Life Books, 1998)
- *Molly's Cook Book* (Pleasant Company Publications, 1994)
- *Molly's Craft Book* (Pleasant Company Publications, 1994)
- *Museum of Tolerance*
  www.wiesenthal.com/mot
  This site features profiles of children of the Holocaust.
- *Powers of Persuasion—Poster Art of World War II*
  www.mara.gov/education/teaching/posters/poster.html
  Includes striking World War II American propaganda posters and companion lesson.
- *The Usborne History of the Twentieth Century* by Christina Hopkinson (Usborne, 1993)

Time Line

1914 World War I begins

1915 German U-boats sink the *Lusitania*

1917 United States enters World War I

1918 World War I ends

1920 Nineteenth Amendment ratified

1929 Stock market crashes

1932 Franklin D. Roosevelt elected president

1933 Adolf Hitler becomes German chancellor

1939 World War II begins

1941 Japan bombs Pearl Harbor; United States enters World War II

1945 United States drops atomic bombs on Hiroshima and Nagasaki in Japan; World War II ends; United Nations founded

Kids Contribute to the War Effort

American kids in World War II played a big part in the Allies' victory. Rubber, paper, and metal were just a few of the things in short supply. Children rounded up old tires, sneakers, and garden hoses, and collected paper and scrap metal. These things were recycled for the war effort. Girls and boys even donated their metal toys! By buying and selling War Stamps and Bonds, they helped raise billions of dollars to buy vehicles and equipment for soldiers. World War II truly was won by the hard work of all Americans.

Victory Pin

To show support for the war, folks on the home front wore pins featuring a *V* for victory. There were many types of V-pins, some of them home-made. Students can show their spirit by making and wearing V-pins of their own.

What to Do

Provide a copy of the reproducible directions to each student, along with a variety of decorative materials. Explain that V-pins can look any way kids want them to—the only requirement is that they feature the letter *V*. So encourage students to be creative. Actual V-pins varied from the very plain to those featuring costume jewels, eagles, soldiers, even shell casings! The size of V-pins also varied greatly, but for the purposes of this activity, it's best to make the pins at least two inches in height. (An alternative to making a cardboard pin is to use self-hardening clay, which can be painted or decorated as well.)

What You Need for Each Student:
- copy of directions, page 67
- thin cardboard
- scissors
- pencil
- glue
- items to decorate the pin: ribbon, scrap fabric, sequins, beads, glitter, fake "jewels," plastic confetti
- waxed paper
- small safety pin
- tape

Parachute Toy

Parachutes floating to the ground meant the arrival of soldiers and supplies. But they could also mean that planes had been shot down and those aboard had escaped, thanks to their silk chutes. Either way, the parachute was a symbol of World War II. Students can make parachutes that are not only fun to play with but that also teach a lesson in physics.

What to Do

Provide students with a copy of the reproducible directions, as well as the necessary supplies. Before they go to step 4—trying their parachute toy—encourage them to think about how it works. Once they have had a chance to experiment, comparing how fast the toy falls to the speed of the bottle cap falling, allow time for students to share their ideas with the class. Then explain that the parachute works because the large surface of the chute "catches" on the air, slowing its descent. In contrast, without the chute, the bottle cap plummets because it is more aerodynamic and slips through the air easily compared with the very unaerodynamic parachute material.

What You Need for Each Student:
- copy of directions, page 67
- paper napkin
- plastic bottle cap
- string
- scissors
- tape
- markers or rubber stamps and ink pads

Victory Pin

Directions

1. Draw a *V* on thin cardboard and cut it out. The wider the letter, the easier it is to decorate. Glue on ribbon, sequins, glitter, beads, or any other decoration and let dry. Be careful not to use too much glue. To keep the pin flat while it dries, cover it with waxed paper and place a heavy book on top.

2. Turn the pin over and glue on a small safety pin. (Very large pins may require two safety pins to hold them securely in place.) Glue the back of the pin to the cardboard so that the pin opens out, as shown. Use a small piece of tape to hold the safety pin upright until it dries.

3. Put on your V-pin and show off your patriotism!

What You Need:
- thin cardboard
- scissors
- pencil
- glue
- items to decorate the pin: ribbon, scrap fabric, sequins, beads, glitter, fake "jewels," plastic confetti
- waxed paper
- small safety pin
- tape

Parachute Toy

Directions

1. Unfold the napkin completely. Use markers to draw a patriotic design on the napkin, or if you have appropriate rubber stamps and ink pads, stamp a design.

2. Cut four 16-inch pieces of string. Tie a piece of string to each corner of the open napkin and knot it.

3. Pick up the napkin by the center so that the design is on the outside and the strings dangle beneath. Gather the ends of the string and tape them inside the bottle cap.

4. Hold the parachute as shown and drop it from the top of a stairway or another place where there's enough room for it to open and float to the ground.

5. Next, drop a bottle cap that isn't attached to a parachute and see how quickly it falls.

6. Which one falls at a faster rate of speed? Why do you think this happens?

What You Need:
- paper napkin
- plastic bottle cap
- string
- scissors
- tape
- markers or rubber stamps and ink pads

Hold here to drop.

Tie a string to each corner.

Tape ends of all strings inside cap.

Kick the Can

Kick the can was a Depression-era game. It can be played almost anywhere with open space and trees, buildings, or other places to hide.

What You Need for a Group of 10 Players:

- clean, empty soda or food can
- chalk or athletic cones to mark a playing circle

What to Do

1. Mark a large circle on the pavement with chalk or in the grass with cones. The circle should be about 10–15 feet across. Place the can inside the circle and choose someone to be It.

2. With eyes closed, It counts to 100 while the other players run and hide. When finished counting, It opens his or her eyes and searches for the other players. If It spies a player, he or she calls out that person's name and location, and the two race back to the circle. If It reaches the circle first, he or she is now free to hunt for other players, and the "caught" player must stay in the circle. If the caught player reaches the circle ahead of It, he or she kicks the can out of the circle, shouts "U," then runs off to hide again. It must replace the can. Other players not yet found by It may also try to kick the can out of the circle. If this happens, all the captured players are free to hide again, and It must retrieve the can and start over. The next time any player kicks out the can, he or she shouts "S." The game ends when a third player kicks the can out of the circle and shouts "A" for U.S.A.

3. Kids then choose a new It and begin again.

Windowsill Victory Garden

The demand for food, staples, and fuel brought on by World War II meant that many of these things became scarce. To help ensure that enough food would be grown to feed people on the home front as well as soldiers overseas, the U.S. government urged everyone to grow vegetable gardens. Your students can grow salad greens in your classroom. You'll need sunny windowsills for the plants to sprout and grow well. Allow about four to six weeks for the plants to mature.

What You Need for the Classroom:

- copy of directions, page 70
- several window boxes (or plastic dishpans)
- clean gravel (drainage)
- potting soil
- seeds for lettuce and radishes
- water
- watering can
- plastic wrap
- craft sticks
- markers

What to Do

If you have window boxes that drain into trays, you don't need to put any drainage material in them. But if you are using boxes or pans that don't drain, students will need to add a layer of gravel about one inch deep before adding potting soil in step 1. The soil should reach no higher than an inch below the rim.

Once plants begin to sprout, students can eat the thinned sprouts if they like, but be sure they wash them first.

Crack the Code

In both world wars, the United States used secret codes based on various Native American languages that allowed soldiers to send and receive messages that couldn't be deciphered by the enemy. Since no one outside the United States spoke these languages and they had no written component, the enemies were baffled when they intercepted and tried to understand a message.

In World War I, Choctaw men were stationed in field headquarters where they relayed messages to other units by messenger. Even though messengers were sometimes caught, the enemy could never decipher the Choctaw code. In World War II, the Choctaw were joined by Comanche and Navajo code specialists called code talkers. The Comanche code talkers were assigned to a special unit, the Army's Fourth Signal Division. Because there were not always Comanche words for World War II terms, the Comanches had to be creative. Their word for Adolf Hitler was *posah-tai-vo*, which means "crazy white man."

The Navajos are the most famous code talkers. They worked with the Marines and played a major role in the capture of Iwo Jima, sending and receiving more than 800 messages over a 48-hour period while the Marines landed and took up their positions. The Navajo language is especially suited for code because of its complexity, rarity, and lack of a written form. For example, the same Navajo word might have three or four different meanings depending on the pitch of its pronunciation. Navajos used familiar words to describe war terms that did not exist in their native language. For example, *besh-lo*, which means "iron fish," was the word for submarine. More than 400 Navajos served as code talkers during World War II. Today an exhibit at the Pentagon honors these Americans' contribution.

Your students can experiment using Navajo code in the activity that follows.

What You Need for Each Pair of Students:
- copy of Navajo Code Talkers' Key, page 70
- paper
- pens

What to Do

1. Give a brief overview of the code talkers and their importance in both world wars.

2. Explain how the code talkers worked. The receiver of a coded message heard a series of Navajo words strung together. He did not hear sentences or regular conversation, just lists of words. The receiver wrote down the words and then translated them into their English equivalents. For example, *wol-la chee* is the Navajo word for "ant." In translating the code, the receiver used only the first letter of the English word, so *wol-la chee* was the code talkers' way of saying the letter A. The next word would be translated in the same way, eventually spelling out the complete words of the coded message. To make the code even tougher to crack, there might be three different Navajo words that stood for the letter A. For the purposes of this activity, only one is given. The code talkers also had words for special military terms that did not have to be translated. For example, *dah-he-tih-hi*, the Navajo word for "hummingbird," designated a fighter plane.

3. Pair students up and let them take turns sending and decoding messages just like real code talkers. Children can write the Navajo words, but encourage them to send their messages by speaking the words to the receiver—they'll have lots of fun trying to pronounce them! Note that since there are few English words beginning with an X, the code word is *cross*. And the English word *zin* (for Z) is made up.

Crack the Code

Navajo Code Talkers' Key

A wol-la chee (ant)

B shush (bear)

C moasi (cat)

D be (deer)

E ah-jah (ear)

F ma-e (fox)

G ah-tad (girl)

H cha (hat)

I tkin (ice)

J ah-ya-tsinne (jaw)

K jad-ho-loni (kettle)

L dibeh-yazzie (lamb)

M na-as-tso-si (mouse)

N a-chin (nose)

O ne-ahs-jah (owl)

P ne-zhoni (pretty)

Q ca-yeilth (quiver)

R gah (rabbit)

S klesh (snake)

T than-zie (turkey)

U shi-da (uncle)

V a-keh-di-glini (victor)

W gloe-ih (weasel)

X al-na-as-dzoh (cross)

Y tsah-ah-dzoh (yucca)

Z besh-do-tliz (zin)

Windowsill Victory Garden

Directions

1. Add potting soil to the container in which you will plant lettuce and radishes for your windowsill victory garden.

2. Scatter the seeds lightly over the soil. Just a few seeds go a long way. You can combine different types of seeds in each container or plant all one kind. If you mix the seeds, plant them in separate sections of the container. Then label a craft stick with the type of seed, sticking it in the soil in the appropriate spot. Even if you plant only one kind of seed per container, it's still a good idea to label a craft stick.

3. Sprinkle a very fine layer of soil over the seeds, and then lightly water the soil using the sprinkler on a watering can. Cover the containers with plastic wrap and place them on the windowsill.

4. Water lightly when the soil begins to dry on top. Do not overwater. The soil should stay moist, not soggy. Replace the plastic wrap after watering.

5. When the seeds sprout, it's time to remove the plastic wrap for good. Continue to keep the soil moist but not soggy. Thin the plants so that they aren't crowded. Try to keep about an inch between each plant.

6. In about four weeks, the radishes will be ready. Soon after, the lettuce will be large enough. Wash all vegetables well before making and enjoying your victory salad!

Wartime Cake

During World War II, many things were rationed—tires, coffee, sugar, gas, shoes, even bubble gum. Consumer demand for goods after the Depression, combined with the need for raw materials to manufacture war supplies and equipment, meant that many things were scarce. Some foods and other goods were rationed, and consumers received a limited number of coupons that they turned in to buy these products. Often families saved the coupons to purchase rationed goods for special occasions. The rest of the time they made do without.

But some ingenious cooks learned to make favorite recipes without rationed ingredients. This chocolate cake recipe substitutes mayonnaise for butter and eggs and honey for some of the sugar.

What to Do

1. Preheat oven to 350°.
2. Combine the flour, sugar, cocoa, salt, and baking soda in a large bowl and make a "well" in the middle. Add to the "well" the honey, vanilla, water, and mayonnaise. Mix thoroughly and pour into a greased and floured 9-inch by 12-inch baking pan.
3. Bake for 30–35 minutes, or until a toothpick inserted into the center of the cake comes out clean. Cool and enjoy!

What You Need to Make One Cake:
- large bowl
- measuring cups and spoons
- spoon
- hand or electric mixer
- 9-inch by 12-inch baking pan
- spatula
- toothpick

Recipe Ingredients:
- 1¾ cups flour
- ½ cup sugar
- 4 tablespoons cocoa
- pinch of salt
- 2 teaspoons baking soda
- ½ cup honey
- 1 teaspoon vanilla
- 1 cup minus 2 tablespoons cold water
- 1 cup mayonnaise
- butter and flour for coating baking pan

Second-Class Women
Before they had the right to vote, and even in the years after that, women were often treated as second-class citizens. In addition to not voting, they were prohibited from owning or inheriting property, controlling money, or entering into legal contracts. When the nation was voting to ratify the Nineteenth Amendment—and Tennessee was the deciding state—Harry Burn had the deciding vote. Burn's constituents were antisuffrage, and he was expected to vote against the amendment. The advice of his mother changed his mind—and American history.

Women's Work
In the 20 years after the Nineteenth Amendment was ratified, the status of women gradually improved. Not only were they able to vote but they wore trousers and were recruited to do "men's work" in factories across the country. With men off fighting the war and the terrific demand for munitions and military equipment, women filled in on the job, sometimes performing better than their male predecessors. In this case, the best man for the job was a woman!

General Resources

◆ *American Association for State and Local History*
www.aaslh.org
This site includes an extensive list of museums, historic sites, and historical societies.

◆ *Black History*
www.kn.pacbell.com/wired/BHM/AfroAm.html
This site is a good starting point for information and activities.

◆ *Cobblestone*, July 1980: "Summer Games"

◆ *Cobblestone*, December 1986: "Toys of the Past"

◆ *Cobblestone*, August 1991: "America's Folk Art"

◆ *Cooking Up U.S. History: Recipes and Research to Share with Children* by Suzanne I. Barchers and Patricia C. Marden (Teacher Ideas Press, 1991)

◆ *Everything You Need to Know About American History Homework: A Desk Reference for Students and Parents* by Anne Zeman and Kate Kelly (Scholastic, 1994)

◆ *Games from Long Ago* by Bobbie Kalman (Crabtree, 1995)

◆ *Great American Speeches* (Scholastic, 1997) is an activity guide for grades 4–8 containing text, activities, and audiocassette of 20 historic speeches.

◆ *Historical Atlas of the United States* (National Geographic Society, 1994)

◆ *The Librarian's Guide to Cyberspace for Parents and Kids*
www.ala.org/parentspage/greatsites/guide.html
The American Library Association maintains this site, which features links to child-safe sites on numerous topics.

◆ *The National Park Service*
www.cr.nps.gov
The Links to the Past page offers lesson plans for teaching about historic places, featuring national parks and landmarks.

◆ *Old-Time Toys* by Bobbie Kalman and David Schimpky (Crabtree, 1995)

◆ *10 Women Who Helped Shape America: Short Plays for the Classroom* by Sarah Glasscock (Scholastic, 1996) contains background information and activities for grades 4–8.